Dear Norman

A collection of stupid, funny and absurd emails sent to companies... and the replies.

A.J. Schmitz

Copyright © 2022 A.J. Schmitz
All rights reserved

First Edition

ISBN: 978-0-578-39812-9

Cover design and interior book layout by A.J. Schmitz
Art elements by Freepik

View A.J.'s work at: ajschmitzdesign.com

Other books by A.J. Schmitz:

Buggin' Out

INTRODUCTION

In 2008, out of the blue, I started writing the dumbest, most ridiculous emails I could think of and sent them to companies to see what their replies would be. Some of the emails were so absurd, I thought "there's no way they're going to think this is real." But to my great pleasure, some of them thought they were real... and replied back!

The companies ranged in size from the large conglomerates that propogate the truck stops of America, to smaller niche companies with warm customer service departments. Food, clothing, cleaning products... I sent a massive amount of emails to these places until about 2012. Then I stopped as suddenly as I began.

Writing under the pseudonym Norman "Willy" Frillman, I documented these emails and responses on a website called *Really Funny Emails*. It garnered some popularity and a small, but loyal cult following. It ran for as many years as I wrote the emails... about four years in total. But between work and family, I simply couldn't find the time do it anymore. So I retired Norman and let *Really Funny Emails* go dark, as well as Norman's social media presence.

This book collects many of those emails. You can enjoy Norman's stupid, absurd and really funny emails on the go, with this handy dandy book.

– A.J.

Olive Garden,

I recently decided to start an olive garden in my backyard, as I love olives so much. Black olives, green olives. I really love 'em.

So I was shocked when I went into one of your Olive Garden stores and found that not one of your staff members knew anything about olive gardens or olive gardening! What kind of show are you running there?

I'm sure there are thousands of people coming in daily who need advice on keeping up their olive gardens and your staff is not equipped to help them. I spoke with two people—some gangly kid named Greg and a non-English speaking woman named Staff. Both could not tell me anything about olive gardening.

Please send me any literature you have on olive gardening. Irrigation techniques, harvesting times, insect manipulation, recipes and any other relevant pamphlets you have.

Thanks,

Norman Willy Frillman

Dear Norman:

Your passion for olives mirrors our commitment to providing a genuine Italian dining experience for each of our guests every time they visit. Our Culinary Institute of Tuscany in Italy has been a great source of inspiration and educational resource in training and developing our managers to do just that. While we do use olives significantly in our salad and sauces, unfortunately, we do not have any literature on the cultivation or maintenance of olives. We recommend using a search engine such as Google or Yahoo to find the information you are looking for.

Lidia
Olive Garden Guest Relations

Aldo Shoes,

I was wondering if you would be willing to sell me three shoes (that would be a pair and a half) for the price of three shoes and not charge the full price of two pairs.

After a serious incident I'm required to wear three shoes (I won't get into details but it involved an accident with a five-legged horse, ironically) and I need the shoes. The problem is, most stores would charge me for two pairs of shoes and I just can't afford that right now.

I also feel it's a waste to throw away a perfectly good shoe when someone could use it. Perhaps someone with a bigger or smaller foot than their other foot. You'd be surprised at how often that happens! You could offer that as a special!

Also, if I may ask another inquiry… I will need all three shoes to be for the left foot. I realize that this is asking a lot because it's possible you'd have three shoes without a mate, but I think you'd find a lot of people that require at least two right shoes.

I'd appreciate a swift response as I've been wearing two moccasins and a tissue box until I can get proper shoes.

Thanks!

Norman Frillman

REPLY

Dear Norman:

Thank you for writing to aldoshoes.com.

We are sorry to hear about the situation that you have experienced.

Unfortunately, we are not able to sell single shoes that are not in a pair.

It seems that you will have to purchase two pairs of shoes or visit a shoe maker to have a special pair of shoes made.

We apologize for the inconvenience.

Please let us know if we can assist you further.
Thank you for choosing ALDO.

Sincerely,

Jennifer
ALDO Customer Service
1-888-818-2536 (USA) | 1-800-326-2536 (Canada) | 0808-101-5659 (UK)

 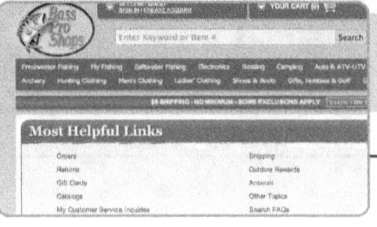

Bass Pro Shops,

After going onto sites such as Amazon, Ebay and Gordon's and looking at their selections, I'm coming to you guys for what is sure to be top quality and best selection.

I need 27 bass fish sent to my home here in New York. Three striped bass, 11 large mouth bass, 9 sea bass and four yellow bass. I was assured by my friend Reginald Stillwater that you carried the best line of bass in the nation, hence the name of your company.

If you could, please send me a quote for these 27 bass, or if it is easier on you, direct me to the section of your site or catalog in which to find the bass prices.

Hopefully this transaction will go well and I will order more in the future. I'm not sure what other fish you carry, but I'm sure as your reputation being what it is, it will be a fine selection. I'm interested in carp, salmon and blowfish.

Thank you for your time.

Norman "Willy" Frillman

REPLY

Norman,

Thank you for contacting basspro.com. We appreciate your business. Unfortunately, we do not sell actual bass to customers. At Bass Pro we sell fishing, hunting, camping, and various other outdoor gear through our retail locations, catalogs, and online web site. I do apologize for the confusion and misinformation that you received. Please contact us again if you require further assistance.

Best regards,
James
Bass Pro Shops
2500 E Kearney
Springfield, MO 65898
1-800-BASS-PRO

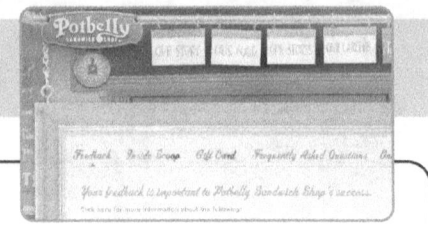

Pot Belly,

My brother Steve and I are HUGE fans of Pot Belly sandwich shops and think you guys are the best in the history of sandwiches.

We first started eating your sandwiches as kids when our mother went out at night and would leave us for hours, sometimes days alone and we would walk to the Pot Belly near us to eat.

We still love them and even though my brother lost all his teeth in a flower arranging accident, he still eats them every day! Sometimes we put them in a blender and he drinks them like a milk shake! Weird, I know, but he drinks 'em down! LOL!

We once went to a Subway and ate Pot Belly sandwiches, which was not met with approval from the Subway staff. We were nearly arrested after we caused a riot in the place and were asked to never return. No problem! In hindsight, we probably should not have started a fire, but we love Pot Belly!!!

Haha! Ok Thanks for reading.

Norman "Willy" Frillman

REPLY

Hello Norman ~

Thanks for writing to Potbelly. We truly appreciate hearing how much you and your brother love Potbelly. I can't say that I'd turn one of our sandwiches into a smoothie but maybe playing with the ratio of marinara and hot peppers to bread and meats could whip up a good thick soup. Either way we love hearing from our fans and hope to hear more from Norman and Willy.

Cheers,
Laura Berrones
Speaker of the House
Potbelly Sandwich Shop

Friskies,

My cat Captain French loves your Friskies cat food! Whenever I even go near the cabinet where I keep his food, he goes nuts! He won't even touch his dry food or his Iams!

I just got a huge case from the pet store and I have a confession to make. I enjoy eating your cat food too! Many people probably frown upon this, but I really enjoy it. I love the Chicken In Gravy with those buttery chunks and sauce. Captain French's favorite is the Tuna and we both are fond of the Classic Beef and Liver Paté. So delicious!

I was wondering if it is OK for people to eat cat food? I've heard that you probably shouldn't, but I love it so much and I'd be crushed if The Captain and I couldn't share our meals together.

Please let me know soon as I'm about to dive into a package of Ocean Whitefish.

Best,

Louise Frillman

REPLY

Thank you for contacting Nestlé Purina PetCare Company.

We are very happy to hear that your cat enjoys our products and would like to thank you for your nice comments. It was thoughtful of you to take the time to express your feelings about our product. Your positive feedback confirms that we are achieving our goal of providing high quality products to our consumers.

Pet foods contain no ingredients that are harmful to people when ingested, however, we do not recommend people eating pet food.

Because we value you as a loyal consumer we will be mailing several high value discount coupons to you for your use toward your next Nestle Purina PetCare Company purchase. Please allow 7-10 business days for delivery.

Again, thank you for visiting our web site.

Dear Coors,

I wanted to know when you're going to bring back Zima. I LOVE that stuff! All my friends make fun of me because I can't drink beer (makes me gag) and punch me when I drink "girly drinks" like cosmos or wine spritzers.

My brother Steve once saw me drinking a mojito and said "What are you drinking, a fucking salad?" then hit me over the head with a chandelier. He's always kidding with me.

Anyway, I remember when Zima came out in the early 90s when I was in school and I would buy that stuff by the case. That's how we got the ladies drunk! LOL! It was all I had going for me as I don't have any ears.

I haven't had Zima in a few years and I heard you discontinued it. Now I'm stuck with those Smirnoff Ice things and they're very strong. I usually have to have them over ice (ironically) with a splash of soda. I get drunk easily. I once got so drunk I didn't realize my brother Steve and his friends had stuffed me inside a tuba.

Anyway. Let me know if Zima is coming back. You can be assured of one customer!

Norman Frillman

P.S. I realize one customer is not enough to start a product again, so I'll try and start a petition. My friend Alejandro is sure to sign.

Thanks!

Norman Willy Frillman

Thank you for contacting MillerCoors.

Unfortunately, Zima was discontinued due to lack of consumer demand. Sales simply did not warrant production. It was good of you to share your interest in this product and perhaps you may be interested in trying another MillerCoors brand.

We appreciate your interest in our products.

Sincerely,

MillerCoors Consumer Affairs Department

Jones soda,

I'm such a big fan of your Pure Cane soda. Especially Cream! I have never had anything so crispy! My brother drinks Coke and that is pretty fizzy but it's too sweet! Not like Jones Sodas, which tastes like creamy goodness and sunshine! Thank you for this drink. What's in it? Does it have some kind of cream in it? It tastes like it! It doesn't have much color so it must be clean. Is it healthy? I hope so, I drank 9 bottles today already. Sooo good.

How do the bubbles get in the soda? Is it a secret? I'd like to know how that happens.

I went to my grocery store yesterday and saw they had a bunch of Jones's soda on sale so I bought 37 packs. What a deal! Is it necessary to add a 's at the end of Jones's or is 'Jones' itself correct?

Now that the summer is right around the corner I'll be drinking Jones's all day and night! And I wont be sharing with anyone. Especially my stupid brother Steven. He broke my back waxing machine and now I can't use it.

OK, be well!

Norman Frillman

REPLY

Dear Norman,

Thank you for your interest in Jones Soda Company! We appreciate that you took time out to write to us. It's always nice to hear from people who enjoy our soda.

The place to find a lot of information you need is on our website at jonessoda.com. There you can find information on our company, products, and our Jones Soda Store. Thank you for your questions, and I will to have to get back to you on those.

Have a great summer and I hope you get that back waxing machine fixed! Thank you for supporting Jones Soda Co.!

Sincerely,

Matilda Ross
Consumer Relations
206.624.3357

Flintstone Vitamins,

I recently purchased some of your Flintstones Complete chewable vitamins for my son Norman Jr. and I was disappointed to find that they weren't complete at all!

They have vitamin A and B and C and D, but for some reason your vitamins don't have any vitamin G or H or K or anything after F as far as I can tell. I checked the label to see if the information was continued somewhere else, maybe on the back of the label, but I didn't see any further vitamins listed.

I also went back to the store to see if perhaps you offered another vitamin supplements with the other vitamins of the alphabet but didn't see any other. I assumed complete meant COMPLETE!

I'm wondering exactly how you can call a vitamin complete without all the vitamins listed? You have the ABCs but no XYZs.

Please contact me immediately to let me know.

Thanks you,

Norman Frillman

REPLY

Dear Mr. Frillman:

Thank you for taking the time to contact Bayer HealthCare. We appreciate your interest in FLINTSTONES® Complete Children's Chewable vitamins.

The only vitamin not included in the Flintstones Complete formula is Vitamin K. There are currently no vitamin types between E and K. Vitamin K was not included in the formula as it is naturally produced by the body, and is also readily available from a variety of food sources.

In appreciation of your interest, we will be sending you a coupon booklet via U.S. Mail. You can expect to receive your coupons in the next 7-10 business days. If I may be of further assistance, please feel free to contact me.

Sincerely,

Eric Marchlinski
Consumer Advisor

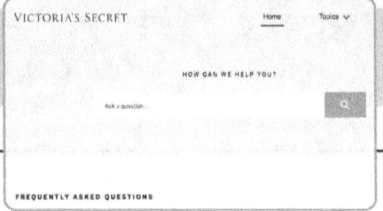

Victoria's Secret

This past Christmas I received the two best gifts I could of asked for. A vintage Sunset Malibu Barbie with a Zig Zag bag AND of course, a Victoria's Secret gift card.

After coming home with my pink bag of Victoria Secret goodies (a black bra and panties with matching garter & stockings), I saw my Barbie Doll candle altar and I had a revelation. Victoria's Secret should make sexy lingerie for Barbie dolls!

Think about the crossover appeal of this idea. It will appeal to Barbie collectors, doll collectors, Victoria Secret fans and it will make a great name for the market. It would be huge! You could have all kinds of styles and themes: Naughty Barbie, Dream Angel Barbie, S&M Barbie… The ideas are endless!

I've already started cutting out some mockup samples from my older lingerie pieces and they are fantastic! Let me know if you'd be interested and I will start forwarding pictures of the Barbie panties and garters I've sewn.

Please contact me soon!

Sincerely,

Norman Frillman

REPLY

Dear Norman,

Thank you for your e-mail regarding possible business opportunities. We are pleased that you are interested in Victoria's Secret.

As you may well imagine, Victoria's Secret receives many requests from suppliers who wish to provide us with merchandise. In order to be fair to everyone, we universally decline all offers to preview and market products from external vendors. We apologize for any disappointment that this may cause. We would like to thank you for your time and hope you will visit us in our stores and online soon to view our current line of products. Norman, if we can assist you further, please reply to this e-mail or call anytime.

Sincerely,

Ashley O.
VictoriasSecret.com Customer Service
Visit www.VictoriasSecret.com Phone 1.800.475.1935 or (outside the U.S. and Canada) 1.937.438.4197 Fax 1.937.438.4290

Libby's Vienna Sausages,

I love these little Libby sausages! I always have a can on hand for a fast snack or to feed the neighborhood kids.

They're great for a party and you can heat some up quickly for some hor dourves or toss them into jello. The recipes you can create with these are endless. Put them in eggs, or dip them in cheese. You can slice them up in Mac and Cheese or boil them in milk wax…

My wife has tons of different things she does with these sausages. She skewers them on the grill, fries them with veggies or dices them in cookies. SOOO GOOD!

I'd be interested in seeing what you guys like doing with these fantastic little sausages! My neighbor Steve makes little people out of them. He dresses them up in outfits (hats, jackets, beards) and then eats them. He just recreated the entire Battle of Bunker Hill, complete with a tiny Vienna Sausage General Prescott overseeing the action for his 4th of July party. He then lit the entire thing on fire, which cooked all the sausages, then wheeled them on a cart to all the guests. Amazing!

Love these sausages and all of Libby's tasty products!

Norman Willy Frillman

REPLY

Dear Mr. Frillman,

Thank you for your email concerning our Libby's® Vienna Sausages, a product of ConAgra Foods.

Your comments are extremely valuable, and they help us make the food you love even better.

We will also be sending you coupons via regular mail that are valid for nine months. Please allow 1-2 weeks for receipt. Thanks again for your feedback. We're listening!

Sincerely,
Christine
Consumer Affairs

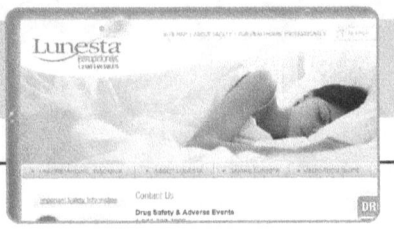

Lunesta,

I've used Lunesta a few times and I have to say the results are promising. After a trauma involving corn, Lunesta has really helped. The only problems are the multiple side effects I'm experiencing.

Grogginess, pulsating gums, swollen tongue, knuckle spasms, French feeling, fatigue, dry lip, sounds are darwinesque, dry stomach, difficulty in walking, walrus gumboot, Diarrhea, breathy, wandering eye and neck pain.

My brother Steve uses it too and he's told me he's had similar experiences as well. Like feelings of having scratchy clothes on his skin, weight gain, hangover-type feelings, remorse, farmers leg, lerching, rusty backswing, knockwurst and shoulder stiffness.

I talked to my doctor and he told me that different users experience different side effects. He said he uses it and at times experiences a dry mouth, feeling waxy, abdomen pain, quakes, congestion, jazz hands, lock jaw and ticklish ribs.

My buddy Andy experiences all of this and watery eyes, swimmer's ear, tipsyness, backlog, neck lock, ludacris, unawareness, freezer burn and "Tom Cruisy".

Perhaps you can add these to your list of side effects. If you have a list of other side effects that I can reference, please direct me to them.

Thank you,

Norman Frillman

Mr. Norman Frillman,

Sunovion is committed to collecting and reporting all safety related information we receive regarding our products and we are asking you to provide the additional information listed below. The information you provide to us is confidential and vital to ensuring the safety of our products and, more importantly, our patients.

Would you please provide contact information for your brother Steve, your buddy Andy and your doctor so we can contact them directly for more information?

Can you please provide your phone number so we can contact you directly? By talking to you directly, we feel we could better understand your experience with Lunesta. You may also contact us at 877-737-7226.

Thank you for your time.

Sincerely,
Sunovion Drug Safety & Pharmacovigilance
84 Waterford Drive
Marlborough, MA 01752
877-737-7226
drugsafety@sunovion.com

Lunesta

Thank you for contacting me regarding your product.

Sorry for the delay as I just got back from D.C. where I hosted a dinner for the 12th Annual Running of the Disenfranchised.

My brother Steven doesn't have a phone or internet access as he prefers to be off "the grid" as he likes to say. If you wish to communicate with him, you can do so through me. My buddy Andy's number is 631-662-XXXX and is available to speak only during the day as he has a lot of kids and is quite busy at night.

My doctor isn't really a "doctor" in the traditional sense. He's more like a healer, if you will. I receive Lunesta from him through the mail by way of Canadian website. I'm not sure of his number, so you have to forgive me for my lack of information on this.

REPLY

Mr. Norman Frillman,
Thank you for providing information concerning your brother, your friend and your "healer." Could you please answer the following questions regarding your experience with Lunesta?

What dose of Lunesta were you taking and how frequently?
Was this a prescription or samples?
Are you still taking Lunesta? If no, when did you discontinue use?

Please list a start and stop date for the side effects you reported:
Grogginess
Pulsating gums
Swollen tongue
Knuckle spasms
Fatigue
Dry lip
Difficulty in walking
Diarrhea
Neck pain

The following side effects you listed are not found on the Medline Dictionary. Could you please provide further description of the listed side effects with start and stop dates?
French feeling
Sounds are darwinesque
Walrus gumboot
Breathy
Wandering eye

Please provide you age, height and weight. Please provide any other medications you are taking and the indication for these medications. Please provide your phone number and address.

Thank you for your time.
Sincerely,
Sunovion Drug Safety & Pharmacovigilance
84 Waterford Drive
Marlborough, MA 01752
877-737-7226
drugsafety@sunovion.com

CORRESPONDENCE CONTINUES

 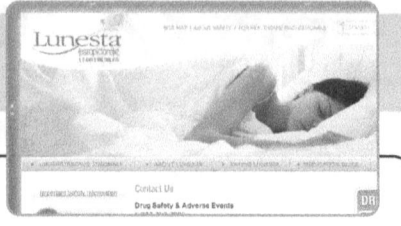

Dear Sirs or Madams,

I apologize but I am unable to recall times and dates of any of these symptoms because I have not been keeping proper journals or logs. In fact I can't remember much of anything, but I doubt it is because of your medicine. That is more due to the fact that I receive regular shock treatments.

Thank you for all your information and time, but I'm unable to continue our correspondence as I work for the government and I'm going deep under cover.

I'm not quite sure where I'll be stationed on this crazy planet of ours, but you can be assured that I will be protecting the liberty and freedom of our country with the thoughts of respectable and hard-working Americans such as yourself.

God speed to you and to myself as I embark on perhaps my most dangerous mission yet—to boldly risk life and limb for our wonderful USA so that all the children and adults of our country can sleep soundly at night—a mission that you also partake in, only with medicine.

God bless America!

Norman Willy Frillman

REPLY

CORRESPONDENCE ENDS

Energizer

My brother Steve and I have a question. How many D batteries does it take to electrocute someone? Not to death, but to give them a painful shock?

I realize you're not supposed to eat batteries. But if you eat even the small ones for like games, watches and hearing aids, is brutal diarrhea a normal reaction?

My brother thinks he ate one, but he can't be sure as his sight is very poor. While in the army he was required to stare at the sun a lot (they called him the human compass) and since then he mistakes things for other things. How long would it take to digest? I told him pretty quickly, but he's nervous as his bowels have been very irritable. That could be for many reasons, but we're trying to retrace our steps.

It's quite possible he may have eaten a comb, but it's unclear at this point.

Any questions answered would be appreciated.

Thanks!

Norman "Willy" Frillman

Dear Norman,

Thank you for contacting Energizer and for bringing this situation to our attention. I apologize you experienced a problem with our batteries.

We would like to speak with you further regarding this matter. Please call 1-800-383-7323 and Reference Case ID: 3103833

Again, thank you for bringing this to our attention. We look forward to assisting you further.

Energizer Consumer Relations

1-800-383-7323

batteryinfo@energizersales.com

www.energizer.com

http://data.energizer.com/

Glad,

I wanted to write to say how disappointed I am over you Glad Zip Lock Bags. I had purchased a box of 100 zip lock bags and I'm positive that there were only 99 bags. I know this because I'm a compulsive counter and I notice these things. A bit of a savant, if you will. Not an idiot savant! I don't like that term.

Please don't make fun of me or call me Rainman or George W or anything like that. I've heard them all and that can be very cruel. I just have a thing for counting.

I use your bags for so many things like Salisbury Steak leftovers, extra screws, broken cookies, peanut brittle and for holding certain chowders.

Perhaps you can send me the extra bag in the mail? I get very upset when things are not complete. There's something that triggers in my head and I feel unfulfilled or empty if the process is not complete. I have been eating rubber bands to fulfill me until I get the bag, so perhaps you can get it to me soon.

Most appreciated,

Norman Willy Frillman

 **REPLY**

Dear Mr. Frillman,

Thank you for contacting us about your Glad Storage Bags. We always appreciate hearing from our customers.

We're sorry to hear that the box was underfilled. Please be assured that this is very unusual and we would not expect this to occur. We are happy to send a coupon and you should receive it within 7-10 business days. We certainly hope you will continue to use and have confidence in our products.

Again, thank you for contacting us.

Sincerely,

Michelle Johnson
Consumer Response Representative
Consumer Services

Dear Dummie Books,

I recently purchased a Dummies book on how to use computers and I realize after reading through some of the book that I don't really understand how to use your Dummies Books.

Do you have a Dummies book on how to properly use Dummies books? If you do not, perhaps it is something I can try and write when I've figured out how to properly use the books.

My brother Steve bought a book on fitness stuff and he's struggling to understand the Dummies format as well.

Thank you for any help.

Norman "Willy" Frillman

REPLY

Norman,

No I apologize, we do not have a book on how to read a "For Dummies" book.

Thank you,

Jennifer

Omaha,

I recently tried your beef jerky and I have to say it is the tastiest beef jerky I ever had! It is so flavorful and salty. I'm not supposed to eat too much salt because my doctor said it's bad for my bleeding pancreas, but once in a while a little salt is OK. I love the teriyaki flavor! Leathery good! That doesn't sound like a compliment, but it is! How do you make it so good? What kind of meat do you use? Is it cow meat? What kind of cows? What parts?

Sorry for all the questions, I am just so enthusiastic about this jerky! I would eat it for every meal, but my wife says that you can't eat jerky at every meal and asked her WHY? She didn't answer me, but she doesn't answer me when I ask her lots of questions, like when I asked her what happened to the good silver that we got as a wedding gift. It doesn't matter. I sneak out to the backyard and chew on a few salty strips after I have her awful dinners anyway! LOL!!!

Anyway, thanks for this awesome jerky. I look forward to eating it all the time and will be getting more soon. I will get some for my brother Steve as well. He lost his teeth in a dwarf tossing incident, but I told him he can suck on this jerky and still enjoy it.

All the best!

Norman Willy Frillman

Dear Mr. Frillman,

Thank you for contacting us. We apologize for any inconvenience. Our beef jerky is made from the "eye of round" part of the cow.

If we can be of further assistance, please feel free to contact us viaemail or by phone at 1-800-329-6500.

Sincerely,

Julie Davis
Omaha Steaks Customer Care

Bed Bath & Beyond,

I've never shopped in your stores before and since you have everything Beyond the Bed and Bath, I was wondering what Boating items you have for sale. My friend Sergio says you have a good selection. I want to start prepping my boat, The Tipsy Skipper II for this upcoming season and I need to get it ship shape. LOL!

I'm in need of barnacle manipulators, hull spray, deck wash, rudder grease, hatch batteners, depth gaugers (for diver spearing), Cousteau paste, Ben Gardner Bait, high waters, wrangle gloves, meat net, shark crackers and a spatula.

Let me know if you can help fish up these items and I'll pay by credit card as soon as the order is fulfilled.

Thank you so much!

Norman Frillman

Hello Norman Frillman,

Thank you for the e-mail. We sell products for the bedroom, bathroom, kitchen and other items for the household. We do not sell boating supply items, and recommend that you try a boating supply store for the items that you have listed.

If you have any questions, feel free to e-mail us at Customer.Service@bedbath.com or by calling our 24 hour, eService Center at 1-800-462-3966.

Sincerely,

Asaan
Customer Service Representative
Bed Bath & Beyond
1-800-462-3966
www.bedbathandbeyond.com

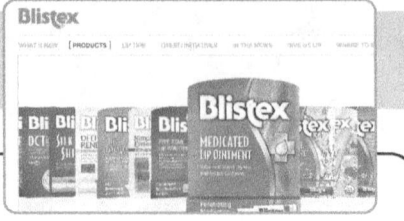

Blistex

After a debilitating popsicle incident in which I needed a full lip transplant (Fist one in New York!) I'm able to use Blistex again and I'm so happy. It's my favorite!

My doctors told me I could use only Blistex Herbal Answer Lip Balm and it's been a real treat! Thank you for making this and thank you for all your fine products. My brother Steve says that he uses those Fruit Smoothies Lip Balms and he raves about them. He has a glass eye so his lips are not affected, so he's able to enjoy them completely.

After a few more skin grafts and some rehab in the gym, I'll be able to fully enjoy the Fruit Smoothies Lip Balms. Perhaps by then you'll have some more flavors; some of my favorites like banana and fig.

Thanks!

Norman Frillman

REPLY

Dear Norman,

Thank you for your comments regarding the Blistex Herbal Answer that you have been able to use and the Fruit Smoothies that your brother uses. We are pleased to hear that you both enjoy using our products and they have made a difference and touched your lives in a positive way!

At Blistex, we take great pride in the products we manufacture and distribute, and we love hearing feedback and comments from consumers like you. We sincerely appreciate your comments and we wish you well as you recover from the full lip transplant.

In appreciation for your continued support of Blistex products, we would be pleased to mail you a couple complimentary tube of the Herbal Answer Lip Balm to use while you recover; however, your email did not provide a complete mailing address.

If we can be of any further assistance, please feel free to contact me direct.

Best regards,

Mona Palmer
Consumer Affairs Representative
Blistex Inc.
1800 Swift Drive
Oak Brook, IL 60523
Phone: 888-784-2472 x3522

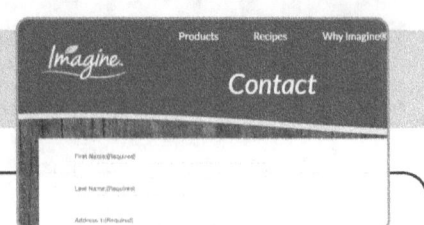

Imagine Broths,

I just finished making a batch of my famous spicy chicken noodle soup with sea urchin and my girlfriend flipped for it! Using Imagine chicken broth, of course! Next I plan to make her my amazing cream of moose knuckle bisque and it got me thinking about other kinds of broths you could offer.

How about camel? Or ostrich? You could have broth of moose, wombat, shark, French hen, mink, whale, alligator, pheasant, zebra, octopus, the options are endless!

I spent 14 years in the Canadian jungles and I have a whole book of fabulous soup recipes and they require some interesting ingredients. Having a variety of broths to choose from would be fantastic. Broths like bear, goat, badger, snake and owl would really come in handy!

If you're interested in some of my recipes (boar tusk & tomato stew, Potato leech) don't be afraid to contact me at any time. I'd be happy to give them to you free, that way when you do offer different broth varieties you can put my recipes right on the carton.

OK thanks! Happy eating!

Norman "Willy" Frillman

REPLY

Dear Mr. Frillman,

Thank you for taking the time to contact us regarding our Imagine Soup. We strive to maintain the highest quality products and appreciate your patronage.

We appreciate your interest in our company and products, and we're grateful for your support. We include all suggestions in a monthly report to our Leadership Team. We thank you for your time and effort.

Sincerely,

Christina
Consumer Relations Representative

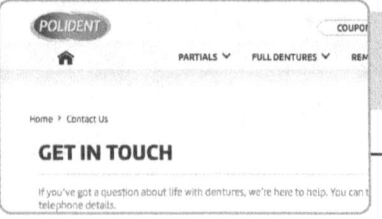

Poligrip,

I've been using your cream for only a short time and I like it very much. I'm actually a younger man who lost his teeth in a deli slicer incident and I'm required to wear dentures until my mouth and cheekbone can be reconstructed.

I have a question about the strength of your product. One evening after a night of drinking with my brother Steve, we both fell asleep on the couch and awoke to find my dentures stuck to his forehead. They were really on there pretty good. Almost like cement. We tried to pry them off but it did no good.

We eventually used steam to loosen them up and then knocked them off with a ball peen hammer.

My question is if you've ever heard of an interaction with alcohol causing your product to form this strong of a bond? It was almost as if someone had glued it to his forehead. Any information would be great.

Thanks!

Norman Frillman

REPLY

Dear Mr. Frillman,

We have received your e-mail message regarding Super Poligrip® Denture Adhesive.

We have not tested the impact of alcohol on Super Poligrip. We appreciate your taking the time to contact us.

Respectfully,
Gimena
GlaxoSmithKline Consumer Healthcare

 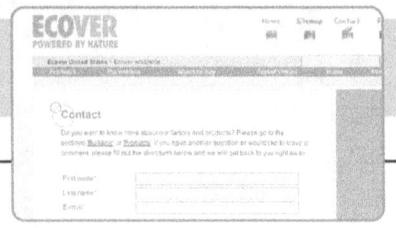

Ecover toilet cleaner

Thank you so much for making plant based products that are good for our environment! My hippie neighbor Janice who lives next door has really been helping me go green recently and I love her and your toilet bowl cleaner for that!

My brother Steve was at my place a few days ago and he alone contributes to half the Earth's toxic wastes all on his own! I love my brother, but he's a complete and total slob with a total disregard for the way he lives and how he leaves the world. I guess it's my job to carry the load!

He stopped by my place after entering a mini pulled-pork sandwich competition (in which he came in third) and proceeded to foul my bathroom like some kind of zoo animal! He said he ate 87 sandwiches. Can you image what the first place contestant must have eaten??? He was in there for three and a half hours, then left to go on a date. Once again, I was left to clean up his mess.

With the help of Janice (a saint!) we tackled the bathroom and did it while smiling at mother earth!

Please send a hearty "hello" to all the staff and tell them "Wonderful Job"!!!

Love,

Norman Frillman

Hi Norman,

Wow! You and your neighbor are definitely a pair of troopers! We're glad Ecover got the job done or else you all may still be suffering!

Thanks for letting us know how well it worked for you, it definitely stirred a laugh here at the office. =)

If you'd like to read more on Ecover and our products, visit our website – www.ecover.com/us/en plus enjoy some printable coupons at www.ecovercoupons.com.

If you may have any further curiosities, please don't hesitate to ask.

Have a good one,

Annah

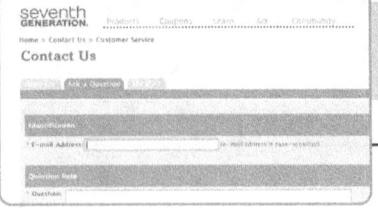

Seventh Generation,

I wanted to write to say that I love your green products and have been using your Delicate Care detergent on my delicate clothing for years.

I recently had to do an emergency tracheotomy on my husband Steve after he choked on a piece of baseball bat, and my gorgeous blouse that I got in Singapore was splattered in blood.

Fortunately I always carry a small bottle with me in my purse. I ran to the restaurant bathroom and washed my blouse in the sink in time to prevent any staining. Seventh Generation is a miracle worker!

The blouse looks great and my husband is happy. It's his favorite shirt of mine!

Sincerely, Louise Frillman

 **REPLY**

Hi Louise,

Wow, what a story.

First off, I am very happy to hear that your husband is ok. This sounds like you guys had quite a scare with this incident and it is great to hear that everyone came out of it ok.

Thanks for sharing your experience with how well our detergent works for you. It is great to hear stories like this, we always know that our products work great but situations like this can't be replicated. It is wonderful to know that when it matters our products can pull through and not disappoint.

I passed this story along to others here at 7th Gen., I know this will help to bring some encouragement for the hard work being done.

We appreciate your support and everything you are doing to use responsible products. Thank you for sharing this story with us. If it can help I would love to send you some coupons for our products, please reply with your mailing address and I will get these sent right off.

Sefton Hirsch
Consumer Insights
Seventh Generation

CORRESPONDENCE CONTINUES

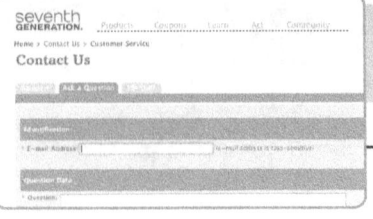

Dear Sefton,

Thank you so much for your reply. My husband is doing fine. He's a big oaf, but we love him! LOL!

That would be so nice to receive some coupons for your products. Thanks so much! That is very thoughtful of you to do that. In this economy, every little bit helps. Especially when you have little rugrats like we do who get into all sorts of dirty trouble. Norman Jr. the other day got into the building's janitor closet and fell into a vat of pesticides. He's fine but his clothes were a mess!

Thanks for you products!

Love, Louise Frillman

402 E. XX St.
#18
New York, NY 100XX

REPLY

Louise,

Thanks for getting back to me.

I just dropped some coupons in the mail for you, I hope these can help you save.

We appreciate your support and all your efforts to use safe, responsible products. Please feel free to contact me if I can help with anything.

Sefton Hirsch
Consumer Insights
Seventh Generation

CORRESPONDENCE ENDS

Bell Helmets,

I usually don't write emails but your Bell helmets are great!

Last season after a vicious tinsel hanging incident at my parents house, I suffered a head trauma that required that I wear a helmet for a while.

There were so many to choose from. My brother Steve gave me his construction hard hat, but that didn't feel right (not to mention having a picture of Mickey Mouse giving it to Daisy Duck from behind). My sister Janice bought me a batting helmet for the Mets, but I hate the Mets. Couldn't wear that either. My father got me this old army helmet from WWII. It was cool, but I started picking up radio stations in my teeth, so we abandoned that one as well.

I finally settled on a Bell cycling helmet and I have to say I wanted to wear it even when I didn't have to anymore. It was comfortable and gave me perfect peripheral vision during our family weekend log fights.

If I ever get into adventure biking or motorcross, I'll be sure to start with Bell helmets and work down from the there!

Thanks!

Norman "Willy" Frillman

Dear Willy,

Thank you very much for your recent email and your generous praise of our helmets. I hope you have recovered satisfactorily from your head injury. I want you to know that your email made my day!

Thank you!

Harmony

Tilley,

A friend gave me one of your hats as a gift years ago before I went to Mexico on vacation. I needed a reliable hat that could cover my head as I'm very pail and can burst into flames if not properly covered. LOL!

The hat came with a lifetime guarantee, which he submitted to you, stating that if the hat ever got ruined or destroyed, you'd replace it for free. It's a bold plan, and I figured you'd lose money because I go through hats like most people go through tissues.

I've had a hat melt when a jet engine fired up while I was visiting a navy base, I've had a hat destroyed by fire when the neighbor kids shot flaming arrows into my yard, and I once had a hat literally disappear when a Bar-B-Que grill blew up in my face – literally disintegrated!

The other day while visiting my great Uncle Steven in his retirement home, his oxygen tank exploded in my face when his cigar touched the tank's flow regulator. When I awoke a few hours later, I figured my hat was a goner. I knew I had the guarantee, so I didn't mind. To my surprise, a nurse walked in while I was having my ear sewn back on and placed it on my lap.

It was slightly scuffed on one side, but looked almost new! After I washed it, it looked like it did before the blast.

So now I know why you have that guarantee. Your hats never die!

Thanks a million!

Norman "Willy" Frillman

REPLY

Dear Mr. Frillman,

Thank you for contacting us and for sharing your many "interesting" life experiences. I hope this email finds you and your Tilley hat well, and in one piece.

Sincerely,
Kathy

Smartwool,

Smartwool has been great for my feet since I started using them 3 months ago.

I suffer from excessive foot perspiration and Smartwool eliminates the toe cheese and takes that excess sweat and moves it away from my feet during one of my epic long hikes. Usually when I get to my destination, I take off my shoes and socks and wring out the extra sweat into a cup and drink it. Very refreshing.

Then they're ready for the trip back. Upon my return home either wring out and add the new sweat water to my pasta water or simply water the herb garden in my closet.

Not only do they help my feet, but it recycles. Go green!

Since I sweat so much in other places- armpits, neck, and crotch- I started cutting up your socks and placing them in these troubled areas and they really help. I use the excess water I collect to wash the floors or irrigate the neighbor's son Steven. He loves the electrolytes.

Thanks and keep walking tall!

Norman "Willy" Frillman

Hi Willy,

Thank you for your email and story (very interesting)! It is a very interesting perspective on the benefit of SmartWool. Thank you for your support in SmartWool.

Thank you,

Tracy Norman
Consumer Relations | SmartWool

Mens Wearhouse

Thanks so much for your big and tall selection!

As you may know (or can imagine) it's hard to find tuxedos when you're 6 foot 9 and 350 pounds. As a former shot putter for the 1999 all Albanian team in 2000, I've always found it difficult to find clothes that fit me.

Recently my (now) wife got pregnant and we wanted to get married fast. She's only 3 foot 9 and yes, we make quite the odd pair! LOL!

Her father and I drove to one of your stores after a bottle of tequila and were fitted for tuxes by your crack staff. They were great and were very polite, even after my father in-law and I got into a brawl (over who has won the most Super Bowls) and knocked over the XL pants rack. There were pants everywhere, but the staff quickly cleaned them up and continued with our tux fittings. My in-laws are Cowboys fans and my family's Steelers fans. Sundays could be rough.

What are your guys favorite football team? I'd be interested to know!

We now have a son, Steven, and he's already a big kid. Takes up from my side of the family. He's only two months old and already weighs 31 pounds! He'll be shopping at your Big and Tall section any day now. LOL!

Thanks a bunch!

Norman "Willy" Frillman

Dear Mr. Frillman,

Thank you for your e-mail. I would love to present the staff of the store you attended but need further information. Please send me the city address or associates full names and I will make sure they receive recognition.

Thank you
Barbra Koenig
Customer Relations.
Men's Wearhouse

CORRESPONDENCE CONTINUES

Hi Barbara,

Thanks for responding to my email. I believe the store my father-in-law and I went to was the one on 6th Ave and 23rd street (?) here in New York City. I can't be quite sure of the location as we were both drinking heavily and I had eaten large amounts of coffee grounds.

We also may have gone to the one near the Empire State Building, but we were overcome by a swarm of Brazillian tourists that appeared out of nowhere. They were all dressed in yellow and by the time we got out of the car, we couldn't even get near the building. The place was engulfed in yellow clad Brazillians and all of them were dancing and banging on steel drums.

I'm not quite sure of the names of the people who helped us, but I think Steven rings a bell. Or perhaps a guy who just went by the letter A...?

Anyway, the staff was top notch and couldn't have been more helpful. Considering our condition, they were very polite.

Thanks again so much!

Norman W. Frillman

REPLY

Recently you requested personal assistance from our Men's Wearhouse Customer Relations department. We have closed the incident based on the information on file. If you have any additional information, you may reopen this incident by responding to this email.

Thank you for allowing us to be of service to you.

Men's Wearhouse Customer Relations Team.

CORRESPONDENCE ENDS

 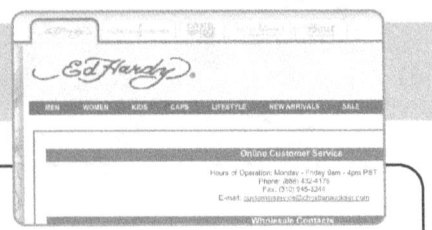

Ed Hardy,

Love Ed Hardy clothes. I'm a big tattoo fan and the graphics look like tattoos. I have a bunch of tats myself. I have a dragon on my shoulder, a keg of beer that says 'suds life' on my stomach, my mothers face on my left arm, my pit bull on my right arm, my brother's name Steven on that arm, some playing cards on my back with the king holding an uzi... I have tons on my back.. a skull and cros bones, shawrnztzengger as the terminator wearing shades and an angel with black eagle wings that says 'once you die you die alone' on it.

I have some Chinese writing on the inside of my arms that says 'life death and in between' and some other Chinese writing. I also have a thousand dollar bill on my left calf that says 'money for nothing' and then I have bugs bunny on my other calf. My right fourarm has a Knife with a snake says 'cut to the bone' a Wolf howling at the moon on my chest. Black panther smokin a cigar on my left fourarm two hands praying while holding a rosary that has car keys to a 1982 corvette on my ribs. Holy cross with a Boston Celtic hangin on it. a naked cowboy chick riding a Bottle of jack daniels like a mechanical bull, Roman numerals MCXII, the Bill of rights on my left rib cage and a 'Death from above' parachuter. a yin yan on my back neck and 'bow to the king' on my upper chest and neck...the pizza hut noid on my shin. My left foot has a devil with adam sandlers face and my right foot has an angel with Drew barrymores face. My right knee and thigh is a robot metal knee with bolt and screws. My knuckles say mamasboy when put together. My hands have a Flaming chicken drumstick on one and a Pot leaf that says 'eatin' my veggies' across trhe other. An American flag saying 'Don't tread on me' on my lower back.

I want to get one more and it will go on my face. Is it OK to use your designs? I was thinking of some Ed hardy designs but I don't know. Have any suggestions? Can you design one cool one for my face? Let me know!

Thanks!

Norman Willy Frillman

Hello Sir,

As far as getting a new tattoo designed for your face, we wouldn't really be able to help you out with that, but you may feel free to get any of the current Ed Hardy designs tattooed on your face.

Sincerely yours,

Customer Service
310-945-3232
9:00 AM to 4:00 PM PST Mon-Fri
Christian Audigier Brands Online Store

Murphy's oil

I've been using your oil soap for years and love the way it shines and cleans my wooden floors. We recently placed a whole new cherry wood floor in our apartment and we ONLY use Murphy's oil soap to clean it!

A funny story… My seven-year-old son Steven loves to run through the apartment and slide in his socks after I clean with Murphy's oil soap. You should see him glide! When he gets good speed, he can go about twenty feet and more! So he did this the other day and went flying right out the open window! It was hilarious! We only live on the fifth floor, so he didn't fall far. He landed safely on some metal garbage cans and got up with nary a scratch.

This got me thinking, why don't you have a sock sliding competition with your oil soap? You could set up lanes (like bowling) and have people slide for money!!! I think it would be hilarious! Maybe do it for charity like the dwarfism institute or Guns for Ham exchange project… Just an idea! Feel free to use it! I got tons of 'em!!!

All the best.

Norman "Willy" Frillman

REPLY

Dear Mr. Frillman:

Thank you for your thoughtful comments and charity competition idea regarding Murphy Oil Soap Liquid. We are very pleased to learn that you enjoy using our products.

As a consumer products company, we are always pleased to know what consumers have to say about promotions for our products, and we thank you for your communication. In fact, other consumers who have contacted us have mentioned the same or similar idea in the past. However, we are unable to discuss future promotion or marketing plans. Nevertheless, we are always happy to hear from consumers who take this kind of interest in our products.

We hope you will continue to rely on our company for quality products and services and that you will contact us again if you need additional information or have any further questions.

Sincerely,

Patty Gorham
Consumer Affairs Representative
Consumer Affairs

Brillo,

I wanted to write you guys to tell you thanks for a great product. I recently decided to bake some bats in my wife's oven (believe me, she's made it clear it's hers) and things went a little haywire.

I guess I put too many bats in the oven and some of them caught on fire. Six or seven of them exploded like popcorn and burst into flames!!! The pieces clung to the sides and scorched her professional chef style oven. Smoke billowed out and really started to freak-out the other bats in the cage. The shrieking was something terrible!

When my wife returned from ladies javelin night, she was NOT happy! She practically staked me to the wall! I ran out and got an oven cleaner brand (which I won't name) that proved to be extremely ineffective. In fact it made it worse, causing thick smoke that set our hyenas into a tizzy!

Brillo (and a little elbow grease) helped take care of any further problems by cleaning the oven completely and making it sparkle like new, without any fumes or smoke.

Thanks for the help. I am now banned from the kitchen, but still allowed near the grill… LOL!

Norman Willy Frillman

Hi Norman,

Thank you for your kind words. We are glad Brillo was able to complete the task.

Have a great day!

Sandy

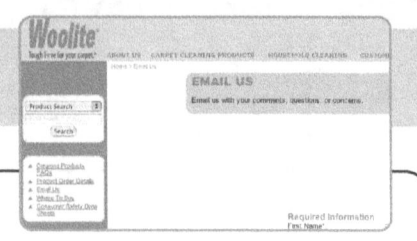

Woolite carpet cleaner.

Woolite, you just saved the lives of my brother Steve and me!

My mother went away for the weekend with her boyfriend Todd and left us alone to ourselves. Needless to say, we got ourselves in trouble… AGAIN!

My brother decided to play with his crossbow in the house, shooting bolts (arrows) at me and was dumb enough to fire one into his foot. The bolt staked his foot to the floor, which he's done before, but this time on our mom's white shag carpet!!! The blood drained onto the carpet in a giant pool and seeped deep down into the fabric. Yikes!

Fortunately we got his foot loose and managed to clean up the mess using Woolite cleaner. It took about three hours, but the key was starting while the blood was still moist! We duct taped Steve's foot and walked to the hospital.

Hopefully this latest incident will set my brother straight, but I doubt it. He's a bit crazy and clutzy and over the years has been involved in numerous stupid accidents like setting himself on fire with Sterno and destroying an original Picasso sketching with dynamite.

Thanks for helping us out. My mother didn't notice a thing and Steve has refrained from walking around her… LOL!

Norman Willy Frillman

REPLY

Dear Norman,

Thank you for your story. We will forward this and glad to hear the spot was removed!

Please let us know if you have additional questions or concerns.

Sincerely,

Maribeth
BISSELL Consumer Services

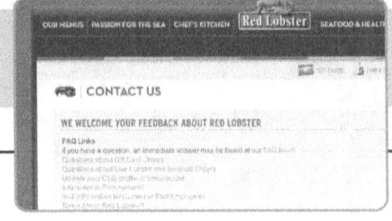

Red lobster.

After watching one of your ridiculously tempting commercials, I stole in my neighbors car and went searching for a red lobster. After finding one, I sat and ate 3 lobster special with much delight!!!

Do your chefs train at a school? Who catches the stuff? Do the fishermen use fishing poles? Is it ok to eat lobster shells?

Red lobster is the best!!! How do you make the commercials look so delicious? I mean there's water and lemon juice and butter spraying everywhere!!! Its seafood porn! LOL! Is there a special company that shoots this footage? I heard Scorsese once shot a Red Lobster commercial in the late 80's. Is that true?

What do you guys do with the shrimp heads? Do you use them for other things like kids school lunches? Do you donate any uneaten food to farms or the homeless?

I really love Red Lobster so much and now I think I want to know more about what you guys do. Do you have a website where you can learn more about Red Lobster stuff?

Thanks!

Norman Willy Frillman

Dear Mr. Frillman,

Thank you for contacting Red Lobster. It is always a pleasure to hear from our guests, and we value your feedback.

We are delighted that you enjoyed one of our Red Lobster commercials. We try to make advertisements that are both fun and whet the audience's appetite for our seafood. Your comments will be shared with our Marketing Department.

We really appreciate that you took the time to contact us, and we hope to have the opportunity to serve you in one our restaurants soon.

Sincerely,

Wanda
Senior Guest Relations Representative

Accelerade

I recently switched over to Accelerdae and I have to say it is far superior in every way to Powerade & Gatorade!

First off the taste is so much better. Gatorade and powerade tastes like armpit sweat with fruit. Accelerdae simply tastes like a refreshing drink. I'm not sure whats in it, but its great. I don't really read labels and dont understand any of the ingredients anyway so I dont bother.

Do you recommend Accelerade as a meal replacement? I once went about 4 days drinking only accelaerade. I guess I should of asked before doing it.

Are there any athletes that endorse your drink? I cant think of any. It would be good if there was someone who did. Since Peyton Manning does those stupid gaterade G commercials, try and get Eli. He'll sell anything.

OK. Thanx for reading this.

Norman "Willy" Frillman

Dear Mr. Frillman:

Thank you for contacting us about Accelerade. Accelerade Gel and Powder products are both manufactured by Pacific Health Labs. You can contact them directly by either calling 800-397-7683 or sending them an email at info@pacifichealthlabs.com

We appreciate you contacting us and hope you continue to enjoy Accelerade!

Sincerely,

Consumer Relations

CORRESPONDENCE CONTINUES

Pacific Health Labs,

I recently wrote to Accelerade with questions about their fantastic drink Accelerade. Unfortuantely they were unable to answer any of my questions and suggested I redirect my queries to you.

At the time of my original email to Accelerade I had gone about 4 days only drinking Accelerade sports drink and nothing else and I was wondering if it was OK to substitute Accelerade for regular meals? As of this writing I've now gone 13 days drinking only Accelerade and although I'm slightly weak, I feel fine.

At first I was simply doing it as a cleanse, but now I enjoy drinking only Accelerade and have lost my taste for food. Other than some mild headaches and nosebleeds, I feel pretty good. I've lost some unwanted flab around my midsection and my energy level is up.

Anyway, I'd be interested in your opinions about what I'm doing.

Thanks!

Norman Willy Frillman

PS: I do also get a ringing in my ears at night.

REPLY

Hi Norman,

Thank you for contacting PacificHealth Labs.

We appreciate your support of our product, however, Accelerade is a sports drink that is used during activity to enhance rehydration and speed muscle recovery. We do not recommend it as a substitute to water or a meal replacement. We suggest that you consult with your physician for any other use.

Thank you.

Tara Hart

Pacific Health Laboratories. Inc
Phone: 732-739-2900 x624
thart@pacifichealthlabs.com
www.pacifichealthlabs.com

Accelerade® / Endurox R4® / Accel Gel® / Forze®

CORRESPONDENCE ENDS

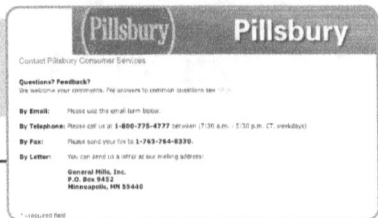

Dear Pillsbury cookie dough people,

I wanted to write to tell you how much I LOVE your chocolate chip cookie dough. I just made a huge batch of cookies and they came out perfect. My wife likes to eat the dough raw, but I told her that wasn't a good idea because you can get worms and stuff from it. Is that true? Can you get worms from eating raw cookie dough?

Sometimes I make fun shapes like stars or hermaphrodites. One time I made one giant cookie from your dough! Instead of separate cookies, I rolled the dough into one giant cookie and baked it up. It was a bit crispy on the edges and soft in the middle, but I put a candle in it and used it as our daughter's birthday cake. She loved it! She wears makeup now and I think she looks trampy, but my wife said that's part of growing up. My little girl doesn't need cookie cakes anymore. She's all grown up and going into 6th grade.

Once again thanks for making this dough. Maybe one day you'll make different flavors of dough for some variety. Maybe one with mint chocolate chips or chicken flavor.

PS. You should promote cookie cakes on the package itself. Carvel bangs you $20 for those fudgy the whale cakes. Outragous! A home made cookie cake is like $2! So much cheaper!!!

Norman "Willy" Frillman

REPLY

Dear Mr. Frillman:

Thank you for contacting Pillsbury regarding Pillsbury chocolate chip cookie dough.

The health and well-being of our consumers is our highest priority. We work to ensure the safety and quality of our products by using stringent safety measures throughout our production processes. Our cookie dough is designed to be baked, then eaten. We recommend that consumers enjoy our products in their intended use. We do not recommend that consumers eat cookie dough in any application where the product has not been baked.

We appreciate your interest and hope you continue to choose our products.

Sincerely,

Jennifer Garrett

Consumer Services

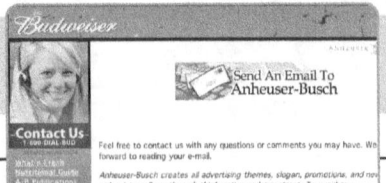

BUDWEISER

Budweiser, wanted to write to say that I love Budweiser beer. King of beers is right! Love Budweiser and bud lite too! Best beer on the market. Better than miller and Coors and any of that other crap! I heard Coors is run by Nazis. Is that true?

On a hot day, there's nothing better than tossing some beers in an icey cooler and sucking 'em down! I was just drinking some in front of my brother Steve and taunting him because he can't drink anymore because he got a liver transplant. Haha! Is that mean?

He said 'if you love Bud so much why don't you write them a letter', so I did. That is this email right here. I love Bud! Haha!

Anyway, thanks for reading. If you have any encouraging words for my brother Steve, you can write them in an email if you want to respond. He can be a real tool sometimes, but in general he is a good guy.

Yes, I have been drinking. This bud's for you!

Norman "Willy" Frillman

Hey Norman,

Thanks for the e-mail. It's great to hear you love Budweiser and I really appreciate your getting in touch!

I hope that Steve is feeling better and wish him all the best in his recovery from a transplant. Just from you note, it sounds like Steve is a good guy and that the two of you have a relationship like me and my brothers do. I hope the two of you will get to hang out together sometime soon!

Thanks again for the e-mail, Norman. Please let me know if there is ever anything I can do to help you out in the future.

Joe

Your Friend at Budweiser

1-800-DIAL-BUD (1-800-342-5283)

Dear Chipotle,

I don't normally write letters to companies, but I felt I had to after eating in one of your Chipotles. It was really GREAT!

I'd never eaten in a Chipotle before and I was a little hesitant to do so when my brother Steve suggested we go into one for a quick snack. My brother gets a little hypoglycemic and tends to get a little nuts and drools when his blood sugar is low, so I thought it was a fine idea.

I had the Grilled Chicken Taco and to my delight found it quite delicious! In fact, if I'm telling truths here, I ordered another one!

But what really prompted me to write was because later that night, after I let my brother out of his cage, we were watching TV and came across a Sly Stallone movie. As you may know, a certain taco fast food place is featured prominently in this movie.

Well, that set him off and he was once again craving some Chipotle and wanted to go after the movie. In fact, he couldn't wait till the movie was over. He kept hitting himself, so I grabbed my motorcycle keys and jingled them and that got him very excited. We drove across town and eventually found a Chipotle on 42nd street and stopped in. I once again had a grilled chicken taco and Steve had 16 crispy tacos.

Thanks again!

Norman "Willy" Frillman

Norman "Willy" Frillman,

Thanks for taking the time to share your impressionable first experience! It's sure hard to stop with just one of our Grilled Chicken Tacos, and I am pleased to hear that you enjoy them. It sounds like Steve is quite the Chipotle fanatic and he has just started the addiction in you. Did he seriously eat 16 crispy tacos or are you pulling my leg? After working in our restaurant for a couple of years, I never encountered a customer who could consume so many tacos (although it is believable with how good they are). It's great to hear from our fans and your story is quite entertaining.

Thanks for the feedback and we hope to see you guys again soon!

Sincerely,

Louisa

Louisa Fredrickson | Marketing Consultant

Chipotle Mexican Grill

Mango,

I was wondering if you'd be offering Native American languages in the future as a language choice? My wife speaks very little English to begin with and after being hit in the head with a sack of kidney beans, she seems determined to speak only in the tongue of the Iroquois.

We've been communicating quite well using a series of hand gestures, hieroglyphics and knocks, but it would be a great benefit to me and our six children if we could learn Iroquoian. Apparently I called her a 'mangy field' the other day and she was not happy about it.

Don't get me wrong, our communication style has been working quite well for the past 10 years and it may be the sole reason we're still together. People say communication is the key to a long marriage, but I would say a complete and total lack of communication could work just as well.

I contacted Rosetta Stone, but they ignored me. Anyway, please let me know if you will offering ANY Native American languages in the future. Also interested in Muskogean and sign languages as well.

Thanks,

Norman Frillman

REPLY

Hello Norman Frillman,

Thank you for your inquiry. We are always open to suggestions. We are currently working on toward adding new languages. Unfortunately, I do not have a time line of when they will be release. Keep checking our website for updates! Please let me know if I can further assist you.

Thanks and have a great day!

Best regards,
Mango Languages
customercare@mangolanguages.com
www.mangolanguages.com

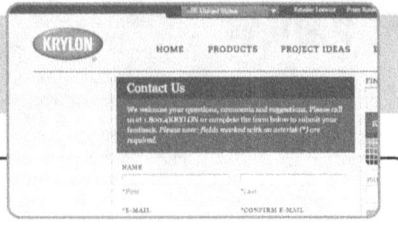

Dear Krylon,

I'm writing to tell you how upset I am with your Multi-Purpose black spray paint.

I've recently started to go grey prematurely. Probably from raising my sisters' twin boys Megatron and Fabergé.

I started using your Multi-Purpose paint to cover my hair in a nice coat of black, just like it says to do on the label. At first it looked fantastic and I was very happy with the results, yet when I showered it began to wash off!!

I thought the paint was supposed to protect against the elements like water? How should I continue to use this effectively without it washing out of my hair?

Thanks for the help.

Norman Frillman

REPLY

Norman,

Thank you for contacting Krylon. We appreciate your inquiry. Our spray paints are not intended for use on human hair or skin. I am sorry to hear you have had this experience while using our product. If you have other questions, please let me know. Thanks for taking the time to write in.

Regards, Kim Krylon Product Support

Dear Petco,

I recently purchased a lovely Parrot that we named Igor and have had a lot of fun with him over the past few months until recently. We didn't realize that the bird was USED!

After a month in our house, we realized the bird was speaking a different language and didn't know what until we had renowned Brazilian, Michalangelo Fezazi come to clean our tubes.

After Michalangelo arrived, Igor began insulting Mr. Fezazi with what he described as foul acts of sadomasocism and repeatedly asking to have cream cheese placed in areas that I don't want to describe in this email!

Needless to say, Mr. Fezazi left our house without cleaning our tubes and we are left without his world-recognized services because of this foul-mouthed bird!!!

What are we to do?

Norman Willy Frillman

REPLY

Dear Norman Frillman,

Thank you for contacting PETCO. We are sorry to hear about your pet.

We do have an animal companion specialist that are highly trained in providing animal care. Please feel free to coordinate with them at your local PETCO store.

Thank you for your inquiry. Please contact us again if you need any further assistance.

Sincerely,

Reggie A.
Customer Relations Coordinator

Hood,

I absolutely LOVE your sour cream. It is without a doubt the best sour cream in the world! It's truly a little piece of heaven. I put it on potatoes, vegetables and other creams.

I wanted to write to tell you how much I love your sour cream, but I also have an issue that I want to know if you can help me with…

I'm interested in being encased in a giant blob of your delicious sour cream. Preferably in my bathtub. Do you think this would be possible? How much can you ship at once? Would you be able to help me?

My wife thinks I'm a little nuts, but she likes to tackle strangers in the street without warning, so I think I'm OK in comparison. I've consulted with my doctor and he said he thought it was a bit odd, but couldn't find any medical problems with doing it. He said the only potential danger may be frostbite.

Personally, I enjoy the cool sensation (I've experimented with small amounts) and it would be my dream to eat my way out of the creamy entrapment.

Have you ever done this with other customers? I'd like to know. Also, are you experimenting with any new flavors? Maybe chives or coffee flavors? I'd like to know for the future.

Thanks so much for your response!

Norman "Willy" Frillman

REPLY

Thank you for contacting Hood regarding our Sour Cream; however, we do not offer mail order service for our products.

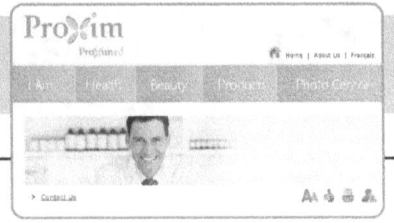

Dear Proxim,

After a having some prolonged constipation I intended to use your mineral oil to help with some relief, but in a rather poorly timed bought of brain freeze, I actually used your anti-diarrheal and I became backed up even more.

So to help with that mistake, I consumed a rather large amount of your mineral oil and got diarrhea. So then I took the anti-diarrheal and became constipated and then I took the mineral oil and so on and so on and so on…

Needless to say this 'bowel battle' has been going on and off for about four and a half weeks and I'm not sure what to do! I can't stop the cycle and I can't take it any more. Do you have any suggestions?

Thank you for any help.

Norman Frillman

REPLY

Dear Sir,

Please contact your local pharmacist, this problem should be addressed by a health professional.

Sincerely,

Leona Veley
www.groupeproxim.ca

Skil,

I wanted to write to tell you how much I love your Skil power tools. They are fantastic and I've based my entire 25-year business around the durability and reliability of your equipment.

I recently sawed off my hand with your circular saw, but I got to the hospital in time to save the hand. Cut it clean off!! The hospital staff said that it was because the cut was so clean that it made the reattachment so easy to do. How about THAT for an endorsement!!! LOL!

I'm still rehabbing the hand and it's almost as good as new. I need to continue to do my exercises on the Nautilus machines and to do this game the nurses like to do called "snap and grab-'em"…

Anyway, I'll continue to use your fine products that have helped my business grow. Hopefully I can avoid any further minor incidents like my hand and make sure to be careful and start wearing safety glasses.

Thanks!

Norman 'Willy' Frillman

REPLY

Dear Norman,

Thank you for writing. I've forwarded this incident on to our Product Safety Department. Hope your therapy goes well and you are again able to go back to doing the things you enjoy.
We value you as a Skil tool user and trust that you will use your tools with confidence and rely on Skil to stand behind our products. If there is anything further that I can assist you with please write back.

Liisa

Skil Customer Service For additional information, please visit our web site at www.Skil.com

Robeez,

We are huge fans of your shoes. My son Norman Jr. absolutely loves them!

Unfortunately, we can't get him to stop eating them. Every time we turn around, he's got his Robeez off his feet and into his mouth. He's already eaten three pairs and is half way through his fourth!

I know this seems like a weird question, but are your shoes healthy to eat? I mean he actually EATS the shoes. Bites into them and swallows them!

Do you guys offer a shoe that is not so tasty? Is there some kind of spray I can put on them to make them taste bad?

Any advice would be great!

Thanks Norman Frillman

REPLY

Dear Norman,

Thank you for contacting robeez.com.

In answer to your question we have no suggestions.

Sincerely, Marlene
Customer Service

Green Forest

I've been using your recycled bathroom tissue and I LOVE it! It makes me feel good to use recycled materials. I have a question...

Recently my mother came over to stay with my wife and me. When I went to use the bathroom, I saw that she had replaced the toilet paper with a brand that SHE liked! (I won't mention the name, only that it leaves powdery perfumy residue and is NOT recycled). I was really angry! I kept it to myself and pretended not to notice, but I was burning up inside!

It irked me that she planned ahead and brought the toilet paper. I had to go to the firing range and squeeze off a few rounds on my automatic rifle to calm myself a bit! When that didn't work I went into the back yard and did some tai chi. That didn't work either so my wife made her special chai tea.

My question is, should I have said something to my mother? Is this a big deal or something to forget?

Thanks for any response,

Norman "Willy" Frillman

REPLY

Hello Norman:

This email is in response to yours of January 31.

Thank you for your email. We are glad to hear how much you like Green Forest bathroom tissue! Although we are not in a position to advise on how you should handle the situation with your mother, we would like you to know that your support of our products is sincerely appreciated.

In future, if you ever have any questions, concerns, or problems with any of our products, please do not hesitate to contact us again.

Sincerely,
PLANET INC.
Isabelle Gagnon
Consumer Affairs

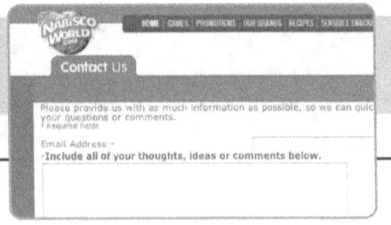

Dear Nabisco,

I'm curious as to why I can't find Chicken in a Biscuit crackers anymore! Did you discontinue this fantastic snack? If so my soul had been crushed into a million pieces! This was without a doubt the tastiest snack food in the history of the earth! I mean it tasted like chicken soup, but in a cracker. Oh I loved them so much. It reminded me of my childhood in Pennsylvania - summer days, sprinklers, lemonade and spin the bottle with the neighbors parents. Perhaps all everyone likes is the cheese crisp crackers and stuff, but those Chicken in a Biscuit crackers were tops!

I will start a campaign to have them brought back. I will start a revolution! We must have them! You guys must get a 100 letters a day asking for chicken in a biscuit. Times change, but soup flavored crackers can't be out of fashion.

Do you have any back stock you can send me? I'll freeze them and enjoy them on special days. Thanksgiving, my birthday, my brother Steve's 3 years sober. I understand if you get many requests. I should not be selfish. Mom said once after church that being selfish is a sin, but I think CIAB crackers are a simple thing, and Jesus says that we should enjoy the simple things in life.

Please tell me if I can look forward to seeing Chicken in a Biscuit on my store shelves in the future. If so I will purchase them by the truck loads.

God bless you!

Norman "Willy" Frillman

REPLY

Hi Norman,

Thank you for contacting us about the availability of CHICKEN IN A BISKIT Snack Crackers. There is nothing more important to us than pleasing you, and every one of our consumers, with high-quality products.

I'm sorry to disappoint you, but, unfortunately we are unable to locate a grocery store in your area that currently has the particular product you are interested in purchasing. We do sell this product nationally, however, please understand that the decision to carry certain products in regional areas is determined by the grocery store. This is often determined by what tastes or type of products sell best in these areas.

It was great hearing from you, and remember we're always updating our site so visit us again soon!

Kim McMiller
Associate Director, Consumer Relations

Superfeet

Your insoles have really helped my foot and back pain and I thank you a million times over for that!

After years of playing rugby in college and breaking my right leg, my left knee cap and dislocating my right hip, I've had troubles with leg and back pain for quite some time. I've also had a few injuries at work over the years where I dislocated three spine vertebra, shattered my collar bone and broke my scapula. I of course (stupidly) still played weekend rugby and broke my pelvis and blew out my left knee and shattered my tailbone.

Then finally, my body cried uncle when I fell out of a helicopter and dislocated my neck, broke both feet and shattered my left femur and fractured all the ribs on my right side. My carpet cleaning business was suffering and my wife couldn't handle it anymore.

Superfeet inserts really helped with my foot pain, helped my posture, and really changed my energy level. I walk almost pain free and can be on my feet for longer periods of time.

I still have trouble eating and drinking, but that is improving too. Maybe because of Supperfeet Inserts?

Needless to say I've given up the rough activities, especially after breaking my thumbs playing volleyball with a bowling ball.

Thanks!

Norman "Willy" Frillman

Dear Norman,

Thank you for writing to us! Wow, what a story! I'm very happy to hear that Superfeet has been able to help you through your healing process. We're always happy to hear that. If you ever have any questions about Superfeet, please let me know. Otherwise, continue to stay well and take care! Have a great day!!

Rachael Gunderson | Customer Care Rep

Superfeet Worldwide Inc.

(800) 634-6618| Fax: (800) 380-2724

SENT

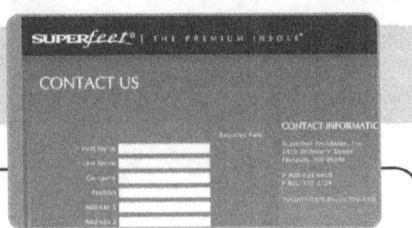

Editor's Note:

Norman's email was met with so much enthusiasm at Superfeet, he got another email unprompted from their office.

REPLY

Dear Norman,

Thank you for choosing to use Superfeet, and for taking the time to share your experience with us. Not only is it fulfilling for all of us at Superfeet to hear how our insoles have helped you, we also feel that we can help others by sharing your story with a larger audience.

By checking the "Authorize" box on our online story submission form, you have already given us permission to use your testimony on Superfeet.com and in our written materials. We would also like to request that you share a photo of yourself to accompany your story – it can be an image of you in action (hiking, skiing, climbing, cycling, running, walking, etc.), or just a head shot.

In thanks for your support, we would like to send you a complimentary pair of your choice of Superfeet insoles! Please respond to this email and include:

- A digital image of yourself [high-res jpeg, tiff, gif or psd]
- Your shoe size
- Your choice of Trim-to-Fit or Easy-Fit Superfeet insoles.

Please go to www.superfeet.com to view all our products. [Trim-to-Fit or Easy-Fit only – this offer does not apply to our Custom insoles]

- Your mailing address

This information is for our marketing purposes only and will not be shared with any other group. Please direct any questions or correspondence to me, Susie Rickerts at 1-800-634-6618, or by replying to this email.

We look forward to hearing from you!

Thank you,

Susie

CORRESPONDENCE CONTINUES

Dear Susie,

I cannot believe your generosity in sending me a complimentary pair of Superfeet insoles! This is unbelievable! Thank you SO VERY MUCH!

I'm going to tell everyone that I see that you are one of the best companies in the world and that everyone should buy a pair of your insoles! Your sales will go through the roof!! LOL!

I haven't been this excited since I won a year supply of Turtle Wax! (I get excited over stuff like this).

According to your chart (and from experience) I'd best be served by a Trim To Fit green insole at a size of F (I'm an 11.5).

This really has me over the moon! THANK YOU!!!

And if I can ever do anything for you guys at Superfeet Insoles, let me know!

Your fondest supporter,

Norman "Willy " Frillman

402 E. XXth St. #18
New York, NY 100XX

Editor's Note:

This is the actual picture Norman sent to Superfeet.

REPLY

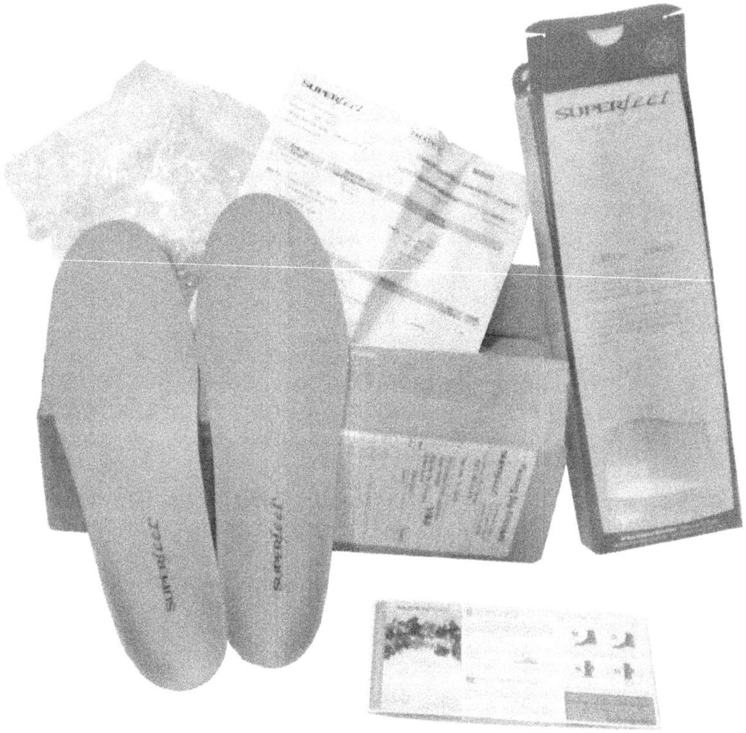

CORRESPONDENCE ENDS

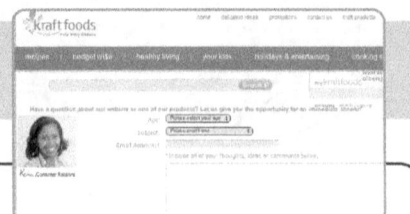

Dear Miracle Whip,

I absolutely LOVE Miracle Whip! I recently tried it over mayonnaise and my mind was blown! Soooo Awesome! So much better than boring mayo! I had an ear infection and I ate some MW and the pain went away! I think that's a miracle! OK, it may not be a miracle, but maybe MW has healing powers. Is that possible?

I've been putting MW on everything… Club sandwiches, eggs, French Fries, sausages, nuts, crispy bacon, wiener schnitzel, crispin glover, ram chops, prawn chowder, sweet breads, grilled canary breast, fried patties, soup, cereal, butter cookies…

What foods do you guys like to put MW on? I'd be interested in seeing a list.

My mother thinks I put it on too much stuff, but I'm getting my appetite back and on my feet again after rupturing both my achilles tendons at a Wii Fitness competition in Las Vegas.

I don't think I can go back to mayo after having this! Can you cook with MW? What foods do you recommend cooking with MW?

My brother Steve said he once sunbathed using MW. Does that sound healthy?

Thank you!

Respectfully, Norman "Willy" Frillman

Hi Norman,

Thank You for Contacting Us!

I am delighted to hear your enjoy our products.

Please visit our web site for Miracle Whip recipe ideas: http://www.kraftfoods.com/ .

Have a question? Feel free to view our Frequently Asked Questions at www.kraftfoods.com or you can call us at 800-323-0768 Monday through Friday.

Kraft Foods Global
Consumer Relations
1 Kraft Court
Glenview, IL 60025

Ray-Bans,

I recently started wearing your awesome sunglasses not because I wanted to, but because I had to!

My stupid jokster of a brother played a silly trick on me that caused me an eye injury. He placed hydrochloric acid and ammonia in a gravy boat on the dinner table, and when I poured the tainted gravy on my roast beef that secretly contained bleach it exploded in my eyes! Such a kidder he is! LOL!

Anyway, after my doctors placed my retinas back in my eyeballs, I needed to wear sunglasses for the next year to protect them from the harsh light. I was usually a "$5 pair bought on the street" type of glasses wearer, but my brother bought me a new pair of Ray-Bans as a peace treaty and I love 'em!

Not only are they stylish, but they keep the harmful UV rays out!

I unfortunately broke my pair parasailing, but intend to get another pair in the next few days! I might even buy my brother a pair (even though he doesn't deserve them). LOL!

What do you think? Should I buy him a pair?

Thanks Ray-Ban!

Norman Willy Frillman

REPLY

Dear Norman,

Thank you for your email. I am sorry to hear your eyes were previously damaged. I think you should definitely purchase him a new pair to demonstrate the maturity level you have. Have a great one!

If you have any further questions, please feel free to reply to this email.

Sincerely,

Mishell

HP Sauce.

I've been to the UK a few times over the years. Once for a vacation in London and once for the annual Give The Dog a Bone competition, but I'd never tried HP sauce while I was there. I decided to pick up a bottle in my market while passing through the British food section. All I can say is WOW! What have I been missing all this time??? The stuff is great!

Since that day I've put it on everything! Meatloaf, hot dogs, cheese, finger toes and alligator. I also cook with it! I mix in my meat loaf for an extra kick, glaze a coating on my salmon feet or to thicken my possum neck gravy.

I love it on BLT sandwiches, steak, lung fritters, hambone pops, parrot bread, whale sack, chicken cutlets, fried butterfly wings, polar bear, lobster tongues, jolie muffins and so many other things!

There must be a huge list of things you guys love to put HP sauce on. Let me know!!!

Thanks again!

Cheers,

Norman "Willy" Frillman, USA

REPLY

Dear Mr Frillman

Thank you for your email.

If you go to www.hpsauce.co.uk you will find lots of recipes.

Thank you for your interest in our products.

Yours sincerely

Elaine Roby
Consumer Care Co-ordinator

Yoplait,

I'm a HUGE fan of your Whips! I seriously can't get enough of them and I may be addicted. I don't think it's as serious as seeing a doctor, but it's pretty close.

About 5 months ago a woman at the grocery store was going for the last Lemon Blast Whip and I broke her arm trying to get it for myself. I didn't mean to do it. It was seriously an accident! I threw a box of frozen peas at her hand and her radius shattered like a well-cooked chicken bone. Honest mistake.

Now I can't seem to find Lemon Blast Whips anywhere in the stores! Have you discontinued this item? I can't believe that you would discontinue such a delicious item, so I'll pretend that you didn't do such a thing.

Where are my Lemon Blast Whips? I need them. My psychiatrist can't find them in the store either, and she lives a few towns over, so I know I'm not crazy.

Help!

Louise Frillman

REPLY

Dear Mrs. Frillman:

Thank you for contacting Yoplait regarding the availability of Yoplait Whips lemon burst yogurt.

We would like to see all our products on shelves in every store. However, as the number of items on the market increases, grocers face the dilemma of finding sufficient shelf space to display products. Retailers stock the products and brand choices they feel best meet the majority of their customers' needs.
We do offer an online product locator, which you may find helpful in finding this product in your area. Please visit our corporate web site at www.generalmills.com and select "Brands", then "Product Locator" on the right side of the screen to utilize this feature. Or if you prefer, you can call us at 1-800-249-0562, Monday through Friday, 7:30 a.m. to 5:30 p.m., Central Standard Time. One of our Consumer Services Representatives will be happy to initiate the product search for you.

We appreciate your loyalty to our products. Please let us know if we can be of further assistance.

Sincerely,
Jeremy Gold Consumer Services

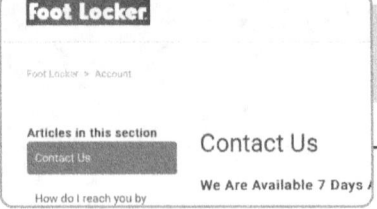

Foot Locker,

I recently went to one of your Foot Locker stores looking for a foot locker and NONE of your stores had any in stock.

When I asked one of the sales persons (I believe his name was Stylez) in the striped shirts if they were getting more foot lockers, he said he didn't know and that I should try another Foot Locker.

I went to three more Foot Lockers that day, looking for a foot locker and found nothing! How can a store that sells foot lockers not have any foot lockers in their store? It's completely ridiculous!!!

Can you send me a list of stores that carry them?

Thank you!

Norman W Frillman

REPLY

Hello Norman,

Thank you for your email.

I have forwarded your email to our Product Specialist to further review.

We will get back to you as soon as we hear back from them.

Please let us know if we can assist you further.

Sincerely,

Eddie V.
Customer Service

> Editor's Note:
>
> Eddie V. accidentally CC:d Norman in his inter-office communication about footlockers.

Dear Mark and Gino,

I have responded to this customer stating that I have forwarded their email message to the appropriate personnel to investigate.

Customer email: nwillyfrill@gmail.com
Summary of Issue/Question: Doesn't Footlocker sell footlockers?

Sincerely,

Eddie V.
Customer Service

To those at Cheetos,

I LOVE CHEETOS! I think I enjoy them more than air or love. The best is when my fingers turn orange. I love sucking the cheese coating off my digits! I got it on our white couch and my wife beat me with 3 feet of garden hose. I dont care. I luv em! Can you be addicted to cheese? Id be interested to find out. Perhaps I can be a case study in a lab. Cheese patient #1. do you guys have cheese labs? Do you try out different kinds of cheeses? What's the point when the original cheese is so good!

I love Chester too! He cracks me up! Every time I see the commercials I instantly grab a bag and start stuffing them down. My wife makes me eat them in the garage now. Needless to say, I spend all my time in the garage. Haha!!!

OK. Thx for reading.

Norman "Willy" Frillman

Hi Norman,

Thank you so much for sharing such nice comments about Cheetos. It's always a pleasure to hear from our consumers, especially when you tell us how much you enjoy our snacks. Fans like you keep us energized to provide you with the highest quality, best-tasting snacks on the market.

Again, we appreciate you writing to us and hope you continue to enjoy great-tasting snacks from Frito-Lay.

Best regards,

Lee Anne
Frito-Lay Consumer Affairs

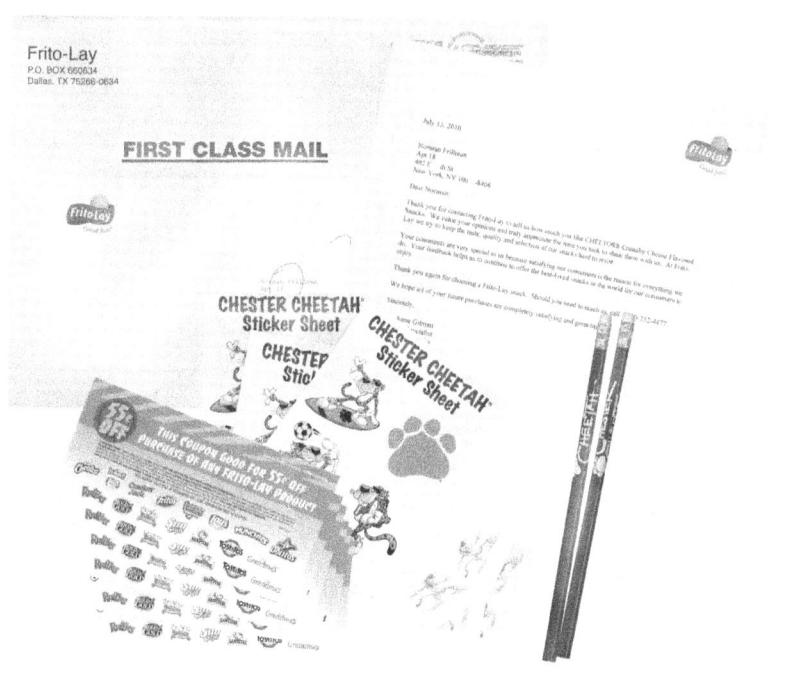

Dear Kodak,

I recently purchased a Kodak MAX disposable camera to take on vacation with my wife to Afghanistan.

When we got to our destination, my wife and I realized that the first five photos in the camera had already been used. We thought that maybe the number register was off or something, so we paid it no mind.

Needless to say that when we got the pictures back, we were VERY disappointed to find what was in those five pictures. I don't want to get into details, but one of the photos involved a nude dwarf smashing a metal gas can on a very tall Nubian princess's head.

You can probably gather the rest!

I'm not sure what kind of funny business you're running there at Kodak, but my wife and I don't like looking at these kinds of things!

Norman "Willy" Frillman

REPLY

Greetings Norman,

We received your note regarding your purchase of Kodak One-Time-Use camera and appreciate the opportunity to comment. Tampering such as you describe would not likely have originated at Kodak, nor would this instance be representative of Kodak's standards for packaging and shipping. Our manufacturing and packaging lines have evolved to state-of-the-art operations requiring very little human interaction. Computerization has helped us insure accuracy and consistency, not to mention speed. If any one package had been loaded incorrectly it's to be expected that a given 'mistake' will be repeated in countless other packages, and we would quickly become aware of it. In rare past instances, we have seen evidence of a film's box having been opened and then cleverly reglued, taped, or even stapled once it's left our control.   To avoid additional inconvenience to you, I've sent fresh film to your address with our compliments. I'm certain your experience was a rare one that won't occur again.

We hope this issue has been resolved to your satisfaction. A Customer Satisfaction Survey will be emailed to you. Please take time to provide us with your feedback about this support experience, as it will help us in our on going effort to continually improve our support. Please make sure to check your spam and bulk folders in case the Email Survey does not go to your Inbox. Thank you for your time, if you should have future questions on Kodak products or services, please feel free to visit our Web site at www.kodak.com where we are continually adding new information to enhance our service. You may also wish to call our toll-free number at 800-242-2424. Our representatives are available to speak with you Monday through Friday from 9 a.m. to 6 p.m. Eastern Time.

Regards, Joven L. Kodak Information and Technical Support http://www.kodak.com/go/support

Avon,

My parents gave my girlfriend, Mláyg an Avon gift card as a gift, unfortunately we broke up before they could give it to her and they gave it to me instead. I used it to buy a ton of fantastic makeup at your store here in NYC. I must say the selection was terrific, but to be honest, I didn't really know these stores existed and I'm a pretty hip New Yorker.

While applying your makeup last night I had a breakthrough idea. I could promote your stores as Sparkle the Fabulous Diva and stand outside the stores and help promote them! I have some wigs too, so I could mix up the looks for each store I visit.

I love to perform variety acts and could do great things like Three Card Monty, a karaoke song and dance routine, butter toast (funnier than it sounds), magic and so much more!

Let me know if you like my idea. Perhaps I will stand outside an Avon store and see what the reaction is by your staff and customers; like a test run…

Thanks!

Norman Willy Frillman

Dear Norman,

This information has been forwarded to the appropriate department for review.

If you have any further questions or concerns, please reply to this e-mail message or call us any time, toll free at 1-800-500-AVON (2866) and a Customer Service Specialist will be able to help.

Sincerely,
Nicole
AVON.com Customer Service

CORRESPONDENCE CONTINUES

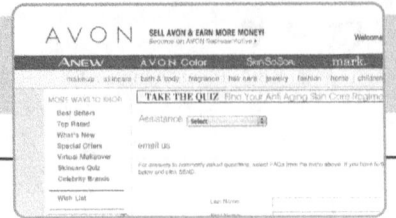

Avon,

I was wondering if you've reviewed my proposal?

I've decided to include a finale to my act "Sparkle the Fabulous Diva" and that would entail me twirling a flaming baton while my dog (a mini schnauzer) Mr. Muffles barks the national anthem. It's really fantastic and I think everyone would love it! Christina Aguilera ain't got nothing on Mr. Muffles. LOL!

Anyway, let me know if I can do this. I have the wigs and butter all ready to go. I was thinking of starting next week?

Thanks!

Norman Frillman

REPLY

Dear Norman,

This along with your previous email has been forwarded to the appropriate department for review.

If you have any further questions or concerns, please reply to this e-mail message or call us any time, toll free at 1-800-500-AVON (2866) and a Customer Service Specialist will be able to help.

Sincerely,
Nicole
AVON.com Customer Service

CORRESPONDENCE CONTINUES

Hi Nicole,

Thank you for your emails. I appreciate the reply.

I'm solidifying the final stages of my act and will be appearing at an Avon pretty soon. I'm hoping to premiere it Monday of next week. I may also do it on Tuesday. I don't have a job, so I'm flexible about it.

I will first have a procession of horn players (Tuba, trumpet and oboe) lead me in while my friend Janice throws rose petals at my feet, then I appear with my dog Mr. Muffles in full glorious AVON makeup and yellow sparkle wig (11 feet high) and wearing a gorgeous Vera Wang cocktail dress.

I will do some magic, then light some fireworks and sing some songs. Here's the set list…

Waterloo – ABBA
Sussudio – Phil Collins
Sex On Fire – Kings of Leon
New York, New York – Frank Sinatra

Then Mr. Muffles does his thing (a tear jerker to be sure), then I butter the toast, then I do a quick stepping salsa dance and then for the finale, I take a member of the crowd and snap a cigarette from their mouth with a bullwhip.

Hopefully this will entice AVON to give full support to my show…

Love,

Norman Frillman

REPLY

Dear Norman,

This along with your previous two emails have been forwarded to the appropriate department for review.

If you have any further questions or concerns, please reply to this e-mail message or call us any time, toll free at 1-800-500-AVON (2866) and a Customer Service Specialist will be able to help.

Sincerely,
Nicole
AVON.com Customer Service

CORRESPONDENCE CONTINUES

Hi Nicole,

It's me again, Norman Frillman. I suppose the "Appropriate Department" will not be contacting me about my show that I wanted to perform outside of your Avon store. Soul crushing, to be sure.

It's unfortunate because I added an x-rated shadow puppet show, which was sure to dazzle everyone who saw it. No problem. Avon's loss is someone else's gain.

I'll simply keep all these golden acts for my personal one-man/woman show, which I'll be performing every other Wednesday night at the Chelsea Baked Potato Bar & Grill from 9:00 to 9:15.

This is a personal invite for you to come down and see me if you'd like. I'll be covered from head to toe in silver glitter and opening the show by playing The 1812 Overture on a 27 foot long kazoo.

Thank you for your time and have a splendid day!

Norman

**REPLY**

> Editor's Note:
>
> Nicole did not respond.

CORRESPONDENCE ENDS

Little Tikes Toys,

I was interested in marketing an idea I had for some educational children's toys. After watching my son Norman Jr. play, I thought it would be fun and educational.

It would be Little Tikes Lethal Weapons: a series of deadly weapons that children could play with so that they could learn to use them properly in the future as adults. Things like guns, knives, rocket launchers and land mines.

I feel this would be great because of all the accidents adults have using these items improperly as adults.

Once the children learn the basics, they can advance to other toys in the series like grenades and waterboards.

I eagerly await a reply about this idea.

Norman Willy Frillman

REPLY

Hello,

Thank you for writing The Little Tikes Company regarding a new product idea you would like to submit for consideration.
Please e-mail your idea or concept to inventors@mgae.com. If your idea is of interest to our product development department, you will receive a follow up.

Thank You,
Courtney Jarrell
The Little Tikes Company
 Consumer Service
 1-800-321-0183

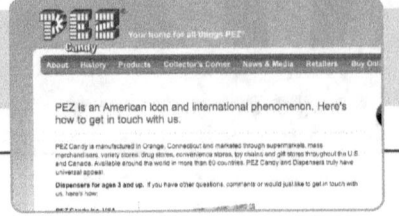

Dear Pez,

I was wondering if you could make a custom Pez dispenser with my brother's head on it? My brother is really quite ugly and I think it would be a riot to have one made and give it to him as a gift! Thanks!

Attached is a picture of him.

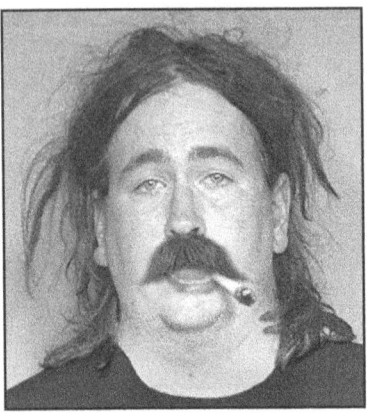

Thanks,
Norman "Willy" Frillman

REPLY

Hi Norman,

Thanks for your message. We're sorry to hear you have an ugly brother, unfortunately we do not make custom dispensers of people's heads.

-PEZ Candy

Fridgidaire,

I recently built a small attachment to my house, a 9' x 9' square room for the purpose of freezing my own meat.

I installed your 16,000 BTU Frigidaire air-conditioner into the room in hopes of freezing my meats, but it has not done a proper job of keeping my meat at the required frozen temperatures!

Now, after a week of hanging my meat, it has all gone bad! My lamb shanks are skanky, my sides of beef are spoiled and my hams are ruined!

Why didn't your product work at all?

Which one of your air freezers can freeze my meat properly?

Thank you!

Norman "Willy" Frillman

The model air conditioner that I ordered was model FRA08EHT1. $610 - 24" x 20-1/2" x 14-1/2" with Ready Select Controls - Supplemental Meat Option - Effortless Temperature Control - Remote Control - Effortless Clean Filter.

Please let me know what went wrong!

Dear Mr. Frillman,

Thank you for contacting Frigidaire and providing the information. We apologize for the misunderstanding but our air condtioners are designed to cool the room. The air that comes from the appliance will not freeze the meat. The only appliance that we manufacture to freeze meat is our freezers or side by side refrigerators.

Thank you again for contacting Frigidaire.

Clearasil

HOME » CONTACT US

Contact Us

ORDER INQUIRIES
Please Call: 855-700-7405
Hours: Monday - Friday from 9am to 5pm (EST)

Dear Clearasil,

I recently used your cream and I was very unhappy. First off, when I squeezed the tube there was a HUGE pocket of air that seemed to go on forever. I squeezed the tube for what seemed like an eternity and nothing but a large pocket of air came out. But that's not the only reason I'm upset!

Recently my wife has been using all my toothpaste as a pimple cream. She says it really sucks up the oils in her face. Apparently, toothpaste is a great zit killer and is similar in many ways to Clearasil.

So to retaliate, I've begun using her Clearasil as toothpaste. Your pimple cream is not effective in fighting plaque or stopping bad breath. Not only that, it tastes terrible!

Please let me know how you can remedy this situation!

Thanks,

Norman Willy Frillman

REPLY

Dear Mr. Frillman,

Thank you for your follow up email regarding a Clearasil® product.

We're sorry to learn that you did not find your recent Clearasil® purchase entirely satisfactory. As a valued consumer, your comments are extremely important to us. Our products are under constant review with the intention of making improvements whenever possible. The opinions of consumers like yourself play an important role in that process and we appreciate the time you have taken to share your thoughts with us

Surely, you must expect us to caution you not to use this product for any purpose other than its labeled uses. Using any product in a manner other than what is listed on the label can sometimes cause disappointing results. In this case, the least of the disappointing results may be the bad flavor.

Consumer satisfaction is important to us and we are sending complimentary coupons to the address you provided in your email. We hope that you will continue to rely on our products (for their intended purposes) in the future.

Sincerely, Cate O'Brian Consumer Relations Reckitt Benckiser North America

General Mills

I absolutely adore all your cereals and eat them everyday. Sometimes I eat your cereal for all my meals; breakfast, lunch and dinner. Sometimes as a snack too. Late night snack, early morning snack. Anytime! Sometimes I eat it dry or with milk or with seltzer. I've even stir-fried it. I once ate cereal for 17 weeks straight. I love it!

My favorite cereals are your Booberry, Frankenberry and Count Chocula cereals. Those guys are a real scream. LOL!

I had an idea for a cereal that I think you MUST make. Since you have the three monster cereals, you have to have some hero cereals as well. How about VAN (illa) Helsing? Get it? Van Helsing with "illa" right in the middle there! And of course it would be vanilla cereal. My favorite flavor!

You could have all kinds of flavors based on ghouls: Quasimocha, Wolfmangos, Jekyll & Lime, Yummy Mummies (mixed fruit flavor), Vampear, Norman Grapes, Fruity Kruegers, Habanana Lector. The list is endless!

Hope you like my ideas and contact me if you're interested in them. I have a lot more.

Norman Willy Frillman

Norman,

Thank you for contacting General Mills.

It is General Mills' policy not to accept submitted ideas in order to avoid compromising our internal product research, development and marketing efforts. Although we appreciate your sincere interest in General Mills and its products, we are unable to consider unsolicited suggestions.

Again, thank you for your interest in General Mills and your enthusiasm for our products.

Sincerely,

Norma Stone

Consumer Services

Eggo,

I recently purchased a package of waffles from the grocery store for a family breakfast this past Sunday morning. My family loves waffles more than just about any food in the world! More than seafood or hamburgers or even corn!

We were absolutely crushed to find that our box of Eggo waffles had pancakes in them! We HATE pancakes!!! My daughter was so upset she wouldn't do her annual Thanksgiving slaughter puppet show and my son is still not talking to me.

I plan on buying more waffles for our Christmas day breakfast and I definitely plan on opening the box first to make sure that we have waffles and not those horrible flap jack cakes...

Perhaps you should inspect those machines to make sure your pancake lines are not mixing with you waffle lines.

Thank you,

Norman Frillman

REPLY

We have tried to contact you at the following number We have tried to contact you at the following number 212-512-XXXX, but have been unable to reach you.

When we receive a report of a serious nature, such as yours, we complete a full investigation to determine how it may have occurred and work with our quality and manufacturing teams to take appropriate action.

All of our products are packaged by automatic filling equipment, and most of our packaging lines can be used to process more than one product. In addition, the first several packages produced after the changeover are visually inspected to assure that they contain the proper food. Although we try to prevent such an occurrence, it appears that this package made its way through our checks undetected.

To assist in this investigation, we would like you to return the entire package to us, including the sample, UPC symbol, and the part of the package that includes the manufacture code. We are sending a Federal Express form for your use in sending your package to us. Please call 1-800-GoFedEx (1-800-463-3339) and tell the representative that you need to make arrangements for a package pick-up at your home. The left side of the form will be yours to keep as your receipt. Once your package is turned over to the Fed Ex courier, it should arrive at Eggo® within two working days.

Nothing is more important to us than meeting your expectations each and every time you buy our products. Once we have received the sample and performed our investigation, we will report our findings to you.

We can be reached at 1-800-962-1413 if you have further concerns with this issue. As a representative of Eggo®, I apologize for this experience and hope you will continue to enjoy our waffles for many years to come.

Sincerely,
Danny Chavez
Consumer Specialist
Consumer Affairs

CORRESPONDENCE CONTINUES

Thank you so much for your response, Danny.

I unfortunately have moved out of my house and that is no longer my telephone number. My wife and I are divorcing and she has the house and phone, and I can't respond. Don't worry, It's not because of the waffles!! It has been coming for some time.

I currently do not have a phone or address to send anything to. My wife will probably not do anything with the Fed Ex box you send as she is basically putting up a wall and refusing to accept any calls, emails or mail. We didn't keep the waffle box anyway, so we would not be able to provide any UPS codes and things like that.

Anyway, thanks for your generous offer. It is companies like yours that make me want to work for you guys. I will check your site to see if you have any openings as I'm currently not employed. Perhaps a quality control inspector or something.

Thanks!

Norman Frillman

REPLY

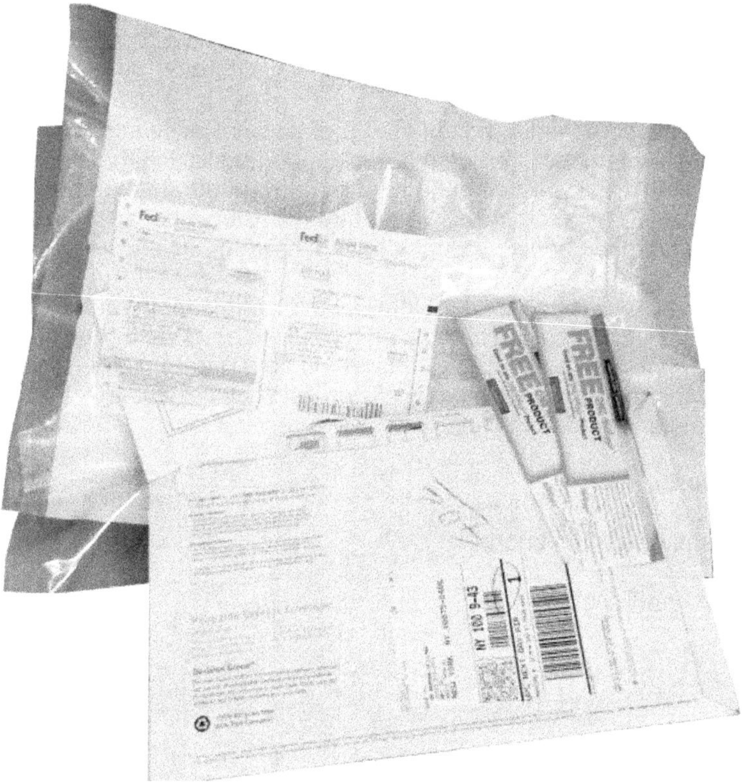

CORRESPONDENCE ENDS

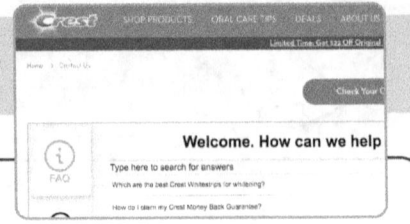

Crest,

I started using your white strips and the results have been impressive. My teeth are as white as Brad Pitt's ass. The results are so good in fact that I decided to use them on my dog Vick and see if I could improve his yellow choppers.

After I used an entire box of your professional white strips on him, the plan backfired on me. Vick ended up licking the strips off his teeth and swallowing them. After he went through the box, I decided to try another box. Well, that was stupid because he ate the whole box again. And they're expensive!!!

Anyway, Vick's poops were totally white but his teeth remained yellow. I'm wondering if you plan to make Crest White Strips for dogs any time soon? I think this would be a great market for you to explore. Maybe for cats too. Then if it's successful, try other animals. Lizards, fish and birds.

Thanks!

Keeping shining bright!

Norman Frillman

REPLY

Hello Norman,

Thanks for contacting Crest.

We appreciate your taking the time to share your suggestions for possible improvements to Crest. While I can't promise anything, many of our decisions to change or improve products are based on feedback from concerned consumers like you. Please be assured I'm sharing your recommendations with the rest of the Crest Team.

Thanks again for getting in touch!

Drew
Crest Team

Nicorette,

I absolutely love your gum! Best thing on the market right now. I chew about 35 pieces a day and it really helps me get through the day.

My kids Chloe 6 and Jacob 4 just love chewing on your mint flavor gum. They can't get enough! They beg me for more and more! I think I'm going to get a case of it for their birthday next year! LOL!!!

Since I chew it so often, I'm wondering if you're going to introduce more flavors in the future? Maybe even mix it up with flavors like roast beef or French toast. I know it sounds crazy, but why not? It could even be a meal replacement.

Thanks for reading my email.

Louis Frillman

Dear Ms. Frillman,

We have received your e-mail message regarding Nicorette® Mint stop smoking aid.

We are very pleased to know that Nicorette Mint has helped you quit smoking. Quitting smoking is not an easy task, so you should be very proud of yourself for this big accomplishment. However, the FDA prohibits the sale of NRT products to individuals under 18 years of age. This product contains nicotine.

We appreciate your taking the time to contact us.

Respectfully,
Gimena GlaxoSmithKline Consumer Healthcare

Case # 3611652

 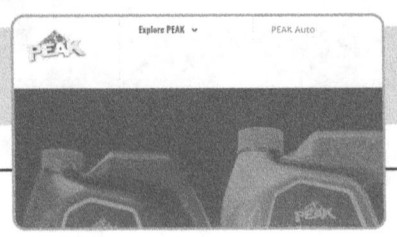

Dear Peak

While working in my workshop, I took a giant swig of your antifreeze thinking it was my cup of Gatorade. I spit it out, but not before I consumed a rather large amount.

At first I felt OK, but then my stomach got upset and I had a bout of diarrhea. After a few hours I was up on my feet and back in the garage working on my car again.

I'm just wondering if there are any long-term effects of drinking antifreeze? I feel fine, but my wife thinks I'm talking slower than usual and my 4 year-old son says that I look like the Emperor from the Star Wars movies (which I think is a bad thing).

Thanks for any information.

Norman "Willy" Frillman

Norman,

If you do not feel well I would recommend seeing your doctor.

Ken Stigler
Senior Technical Service Representative
Old World Industries, Inc.
4065 Commercial Ave.
Northbrook, IL 60062-1851
847-559-2083
Fax; 847-664-7083

Polar,

I recently purchased a FT40F Women's Heart Rate Monitor. It was a purchase I had been looking forward to getting for quite some time. An item I needed.

The very first time I used it (a quick walk) I was shocked and dismayed when I checked my heart rate to find the monitor displaying the word FATASS on the LCD screen! At first I thought I was reading it wrong, that it said FATBURN, but as sure as the sun shines, it said Fatass! I continued walking (dumbfounded obviously) a bit further while pressing a few buttons only to discover the display reading BACON BUTT.

Then after that, the display went dead and that was it. Kapoot!

Perhaps this was some kind of sick joke, or maybe you had a bad microchip or perhaps someone manipulated this one, but I was completely offended. I've been trying to lose weight for some time, and these types of insults, especially from a wrist watch, are very demoralizing.

Louise Frillman

Thank you for your email. I am sorry for this situation but we have never had a case like this reported. There is no way program the watch to display these vulgar terms. Our company is based in Finland where all of our RnD is done and these are English Slang Terms. The watch will display the terms "Fat Burn" and "Cardio" when referring to the Energy Pointer Feature of the FT40. Where/When was this watch purchased?

Please feel free to contact us directly using the link below. We have representatives available via Livechat, E-mail and our toll free line Monday-Friday 9am-5:15pm EST.
http://www.polarusa.com/us-en

Thank you for Joining the Training Revolution!

David@ Polar Customer Support
POLAR ELECTRO INC.

Thanks so much for your quick response!!!

I'm embarrassed to say that my husband has played a trick on me. He's a real practical joker and a computer wiz and he manipulated my Polar monitor to say those things before I had a chance to use it. I should have known! I'm so stupid. I should have gone straight to him before I wrote you. He's so fast!

The Joker (as we call him around here) once put a rabid guinea pig in my sock drawer and replaced my birth control pills with Tic Tacs, among some of the hilarious things he's done.

Anyway, the Polar is back to working order. Thanks so much for your quick response. You may be faster than my husband! LOL!

Now I plan to replace Norman's eye drops with Crazy Glue.

Thanks a million!

Louise

REPLY

Hi Louise,

Thanks so much for the email and letting us know! We take exercise and health very seriously and would never do anything to jeopardize your motivation to be fit. We're very happy to hear it was just a practical joke!

Now on to the serious business... Payback! Can we suggest possibly resetting his alarm clock along to make him get up for work in the middle of the night? Take it a step further and change the clocks in your house and his car so he winds up in the office at 3am!

Have a great holiday!

Chris @ Polar Customer Support

CORRESPONDENCE ENDS

Dean & Deluca

I spent 31 years traveling the east and I'm surprised at my lack of spice choices here in the States. I ventured from the cold mountains of Kilimanjaro through the valleys of Chin Hi province with famed French/Mongolian explorer Lieutenant General Jean-Pierre 'Long Oar' Wong-Merkin and I experienced so many unique flavors that I now miss them terribly.

I started mixing my own spices and I think a place as sophisticated as Dean & Deluca would be perfect to introduce an exotic line of spices and condiments. What do you think?

Things such as dried cricket wing, scorpion venom, spider foot hair, hummingbird embryo husk, seahorse cream, red ant thorax, beetle juice, hornet butter, grasshopper legs, cicada larva powder, cockroach eggs, monkfish scales, crispy locust shell, sloth dandruff, caterpillar skin flakes and lady bug pepper.

And that is just the tip of the iceberg. I'm sure your many Asian consumers would be wholeheartedly behind this idea.

If you'd like me to send samples of my spices, please let me know. I've made a fresh batch of ground black water beetle, dried salmon retina and huge sack of spicy centipede legs should be done marinating in a few days.

I realize the names could be a turn off, so perhaps you can call them things like 'sunshine flakes' or 'tangy powder.'

Let me know where to send samples. Thanks!

Norman "Willy" Frillman

REPLY

Dear Norman Frillman,

Thank you for your recent inquiry with DEAN & DELUCA.

We are always interested to hear of new and exciting products or services and appreciate your e-mail.

If you are interested in submitting an item or information regarding a service for DEAN & DELUCA stores, catalog or internet divisions, please send product information or samples to:

New Product Submissions
560 Broadway
New York, NY 10012

If you would like to submit preliminary information please do so by sending an email to newproducts@deandeluca.com.

All items will be reviewed upon receipt and we will contact you if we need additional information.

Thank you,

Kim Middlemist
DEAN & DELUCA
Customer Care

Mars Candy,

3 Musketeers is a candy bar with nougat covered in chocolate, a Milky Way is nougat and caramel covered in chocolate and a Snickers is nougat, caramel and peanuts covered in chocolate.

Now you've miraculously taken it one step further, and added peanut butter to the combination (nougat, caramel, peanuts and peanut butter) but have not given this treat a new name?

You're simply calling it a 'Snickers Peanut Butter!' That is ridiculous! This new bar deserves an entirely new name and identity! The next level! Why haven't you done this? I'm flummoxed. Dumbstruck. Flabbergasted!

I've taken the liberty of coming up with a chunk of great names to name this new bar you've created…

Infinity, Shucks, Kid Gloves, The Spangler, Nut Sack, Handlebar, Flim Flam, Nutty Professor, The Mowzer, Boing!, Hokey Pokey, Flayvin', The Scooner, Back Lash, Sir Galahad, Monticello, Muncher Cruncher, Ol' Ironsides, The Banger, Summer Dayz, French Kiss, Puckles, The Warbler, Money Shot, Hopscotch, Exsqueeze me?, Melty, Pomp & Circumstance, Yo Vinny!, Quarterback, Smooth & Rich, Heaven Rod, The Juggler, Straight Flush, Cream Fest, Teeth Tickler, Total Package, Shrug & Run, Deep Throat, Slam Dunk, Knocker, Nut Butter, Down The Hatch, Mt. Rushmore, Grizzly Bear, ChocoHammer, Peanut Batter, Elephant Cash.

Let me know which one you like and we can run with it!

I'm eagerly awaiting your response.

Norman "Willy" Frillman

REPLY

Dear Mr. Frillman,

In response to your email regarding SNICKERS PEANUT BUTTER.

Thank you for your email.

It was thoughtful of you to offer your creative ideas. Unfortunately, it is our policy not to accept unsolicited ideas. At Mars Chocolate North America, we rely on our extensive Research and Development staff to design, develop and refine product concepts. Sometimes research and development can take years before a finished product can be marketed. To avoid confusion of ownership, we must refuse the thousands of suggestions we receive every year, many the same as yours. Although we appreciate your interest, we hope you will understand our business position.

Have a great day!

Your Friends at Mars Chocolate North America

MM/ROBIASHL011413483A

G'day Outback Steakhouse,

I recently went to one of your Outback steakhouses because I had a gift certificate and let me tell you Outback ROCKS! My wife and I had the best time ever!

First off, the staff was super duper friendly! The hostess was as sweet as can be and let me tell you, she was easy on the eyes! Don't tell my wife I said that. She'd whip me with her leather leash! LOL!

Then we were seated at a prime table and our waitress swiftly took our order. I ordered a big beer, but when she returned she brought the biggest friggin' mug of beer I ever saw! Talk about large, the thing was THE SIZE OF MY LEG! You Aussies really know how to drink!!!! Not only that but the mug was ice friggin' cold! Needless to say I pounded that puppy in about 3 minutes. Then ordered another!

My coconut shrimp was great! I was about to have them 'throw another shrimp on the barbie', but then my order of ribs came and it was HUGE! So dam GOOD!

Our waitress asked if we wanted dessert, but I had to decline. All that food and 6 beers will fill you up good!

I'm coming back for more so keep plenty of mugs in the fridge!!! LOL!

Cheers mates!

Norman "Willy" Frillman

REPLY

G'day mate,

Thank you for your taking the time to write to us. Your comments about our fellow Outbackers are greatly appreciated and will be passed along to the appropriate Regional Manager for recognition. Hearing from satisfied guests helps provide the valuable feedback we need to address opportunities and recognize performance within our restaurants.

We will pass the word along, mate. Thank you for being our valued guest and making Outback Steakhouse your restaurant of choice.

Norman,
I'd like to pass this along to the appropriate Regional Office, but need to know the location where you dined.

Thank you.

Cristin D.
Customer Relations/Ecommerce
Outback Steakhouse

CORRESPONDENCE CONTINUES

Hi Cristin!

I dined in the Manhattan location at 919 Third Ave. at 56th Street.

I haven't been back yet, but I hope to do so very soon! Those people there are the best and since it's been so hot here in New York City, I can't wait to go in and have a few of those giant delicious ice cold beers that you have there.

Tell them they are great and that they are all doing a fine job! If I had some gold metals or something, I'd give them all one! LOL!

Anyway, thanks for responding to my email. It must be great working for Outback Steakhouse! Do you get free food? Do you enjoy drinking those giant beers there too? I think i may sneak out during my lunch break and have 1 or 2... or 3... LOL!

Ok. Take care!

Norman Frillman

REPLY

Your comments have been passed along.

Thank you.

Cristin D.
Customer Relations/Ecommerce
Outback Steakhouse

CORRESPONDENCE ENDS

 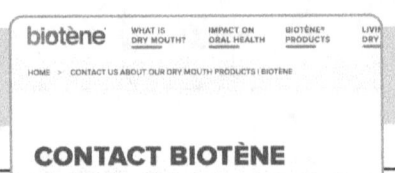

CONTACT BIOTÈNE

Biotene,

I wanted to write to tell you how much I enjoy your Biotene mouthwash.

I'm 87 years old and last year after a devastating needlepoint accident in which I started to purl when I meant to knit, I ended up putting a needle through my thumb and the results were absolutely gruesome. I spent some time in Holy Mother of Wong Kar Wai Hospital in China Town here in New York City and rehabbed with the fine folks over at Bai Ling Mercy.

After I was released, I continued to have terrible pain in my thumb, elbow and neck, with shooting pains in my face and skull. My doctor gave me some very strong medicine, but that made me too fatigued to needlepoint, so he gave me a prescription for medical marijuana and that really helped me manage my pain! Not only that, my concentration was so keen that I knit three sweaters in one night.

Unfortunately, my mouth was so dry all the time from the marijuana that I found it difficult and embarrassing to talk. After seeing your mouthwash ad, I started using Biotene and the cottonmouth disappeared! And it has a taste I really enjoy.

Peace,

Louise Frillman

REPLY

Dear Ms. Frillman,

Thank you for contacting us regarding Biotène Mouthwash. It's always a pleasure to hear from a satisfied customer and we're glad to hear that you are enjoying such good results from using our product. We think it's a great product as well and it's good to know that it's working so well for you. We appreciate your taking the time to contact us and will pass along your communication to some of the other people who are on the Biotène® team. We all love messages like yours! We appreciate your taking the time to contact us.

Respectfully,
Gimena
GlaxoSmithKline Consumer Healthcare

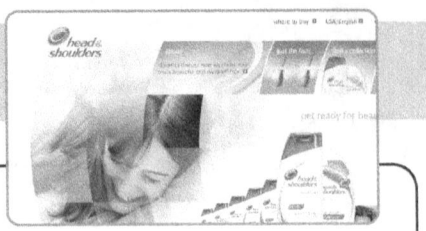

Head & Shoulders

I've been using H&S now for a year and let me say that it has really changed my life! My friends used to call me Mr. Winter because it was always snowing when I was around. I couldn't wear black, or blue or anything dark, really.

I'd never had dandruff before until about a year after I was struck by lightning. (I know, crazy!) then the dandruff started, as did my confidence.

I started using the H&S and it did nothing… at first. My mother insisted that I stick with it! What I didn't realize is that I was drinking it and not putting on my head! I thought it was medicine!!!! I started washing my hair with it and lo and behold it started working!

Now the dandruff is gone and I look and feel great. Now my friends call me Mr. Winter because I'm so cool with the ladies… I still like to eat H&S once in a while (I've acquired a taste) and put it on chops, salads and potatoes…

Thanks again!

Norman "Willy" Frillman

REPLY

Thank you for contacting Head & Shoulders., Norman.

We appreciate your taking the time to share such kind words! The fact that we've made a difference, however small, in the lives of our loyal consumers is the greatest compliment of all. Your reaction is just what we hoped for -- I can't wait to share your story with the rest of our team.

Thanks again for writing!

Pat
Head & Shoulders Team

Red Bull,

I just pulled a Triple Lindy and I owe it all to Red Bull!

Two months after getting out of the hospital with a full facial fracture and spine displacement, I was back out doin' what I do!

My confidence was down, but I was getting stronger everyday. I had broken tons of stuff before - both my elbows, my leg, my tailbone, my fingers and toes, and have sliced open my neck and torn my sack – but this last accident really shook me.

I got back on the board and pulled the triple! I had never had a Red Bull before, and after I had it, I pulled the TL. Coincidence? I Think NOT!

It definitely gave me wings! Speaking of wings, how can I fly one of those little jet plane things I see on TV where the guys are weeving through the cones in the water? That is seriously dope! Do you need a lesson to do that?

Peace!

Norman "Willy" Frillman

REPLY BY PHONE

"Hi Norman,

"This is Marissa calling from Red Bull, I just got your email and I have to say it is a pretty rad story, so I just wanted to call and talk to you a little bit... um... and you know, catch up and, 'cause I know you're a big Red Bull fan...

As far as flying one of those little jet plane things that you see on TV, weeving through the cones as you described it, that is actually Red Bull Air Race... um, if you check out redbullairrace.com, you can get the lowdown on that and see what it takes to be one of the pilots. And I'm preeeeetty sure those guys have been doing it for a very long time.

So, hopefully maybe one day you'll be good enough to join them. Um, but yea, give us a call back, I definitely wanted to chat for a little bit, you can hit us back at 877 673 9444.

Look forward to talking to you.

Bye Norman!"

Dear K-SWISS,

I used your K-Swiss Super Tubes sneakers for two months to train and I couldn't believe the results! Not only did they help me get in shape, they helped my leg velocity for the International Ass-Kicking competition in Stockholm Sweden where I came in third!

Besides my regular training of running, pilates and braunschweiger, I used the Super Tubes to help get my legs in TOP form.

Unfortunately I was defeated in the competition by Steve "Ironsides" Bostwick who came in second and eventually lost to Drake "I Take No Prisoners" Magillicutty, the first place winner and last year's champ. Perhaps if I continue using Super Tubes for the whole training year, it will give me the edge I need to go all the way.

Maybe I'll even use the Super Tubes in the contest itself. Perhaps you could be the sponsor? This year I used last year's Buster Brown wooden soled 'consultant' leather wing tips, but they did not give me the snap I desire... Drake is sponsored by Doc Martins and Steve is sponsored by Jimmy Choo. If you sponsored me I could quit my job at the juice bar and train full time. I'd use Super Tubes in competition and would talk them up through the whole two week competition from opening gala affair to trophy presentation.

Let me know if it's possible to sponsor me at next year's competition! Perhaps my nickname could be "Super Tubes"! I'll be waiting for a response.

Thanks!

Norman "Willy" Frillman

REPLY

Hey Norman-

Or should I say "The Super Tubes Dude"

Congrats on the super success you are having with Super Tubes.

Sponsoring is a bit difficult only because the budget that is allocate for the sports marketing team goes through several revisions then gets final sign-off from the President of K-Swiss, this is now in stone for 2011

But--- Please give me your mailing address and I will send you some K-Swiss gear on me. Then you will be styling with Super Tubes and some gear to match

Thanks!
-S

Scott Shulman
Director of E-Commerce
K-Swiss Inc
818-706-5203 direct
800-938-8000 toll free
sshulman@k-swiss.com5

CORRESPONDENCE CONTINUES

Hey Scott!

You'd really send me some stuff? That would be totally awesome!

I'll wear the gear regardless of being sponsored or not! It's really all about image and, of course, winning the competition!!

K-Swiss is now number one in my book of excellent companies and I will tell everyone that I see that they are by and large the best sneaker company in this or any other galaxy! I haven't been this excited since I won a cheese of the month subscription at the Richard M. Nixon lawn darts competition at Duke University!

I'll keep you informed of my training progress and my status at the next competition in Stockholm. It's fierce competition, but you gotta stay hungry. Only the strong survive!

Keep on kickin'!!!

Norman Frillman

402 E. XXth St. #18
New York, NY 100XX

My pleasure……
-S

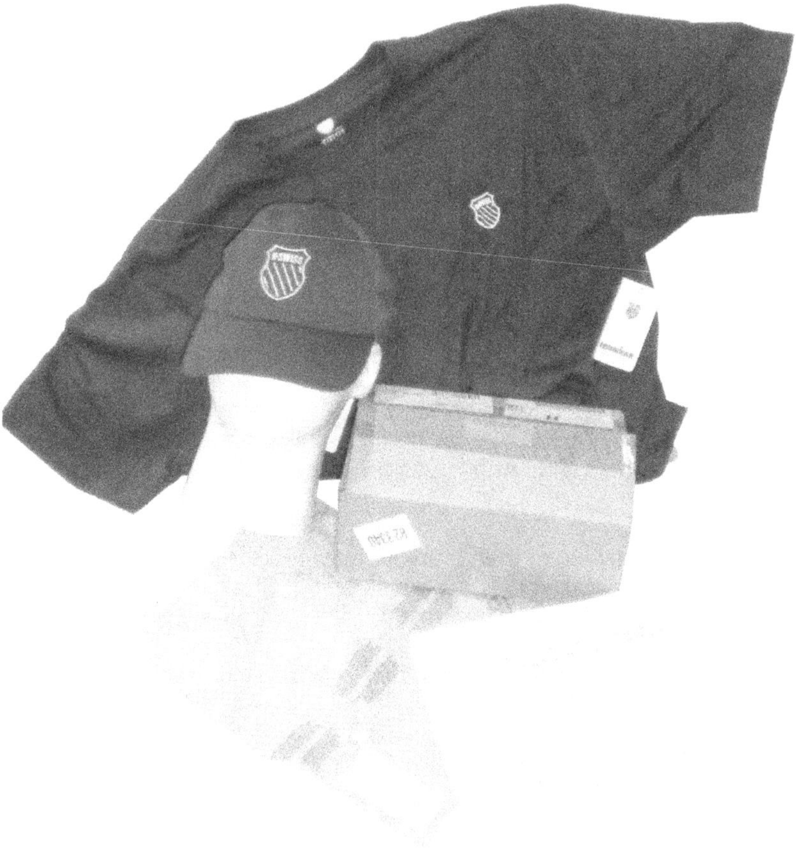

CORRESPONDENCE ENDS

 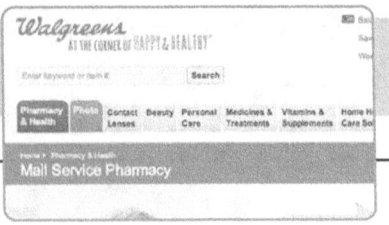

Walgreens,

I really love your bargain Walgreen's products, especially the razors!

I recently stopped into a Walgreen's store that was going out of business. They were practically giving stuff away! I purchased 11 bags of razors for about three dollars! What a bargain!!

I went home and started to shave because I needed a shave very badly as I hadn't done so in about 14 months. I got so into it I went overboard. I did my face then continued up and did the top of my head! It looked great! Then I did my eyebrows too! WOW! I looked like a cue ball.

After stripping down, I did my chest, arm pits, stomach and… "Ahem"

I then opened a second bag and went after my legs with a fresh set of blades and a can of shaving cream. Four hours later, I was clean from head to toe! And it was no small feet! I'm a pretty hairy guy! LOL!

After tackling my legs I then shaved my wife. She was upset at first because I did it while she was sleeping. She's gotten used to it now and actually loves the feeling.

Our kids think we're nuts, but we don't care. We're bald and beautiful!!!

Long live Walgreen's razors!

Norman "Willy" Frillman

REPLY

Dear Norman,

Thank you for taking the time to contact us. We are always interested to hear from our customers and were happy to learn that you are pleased with our Walgreens brand Razors.

For more than 100 years, Walgreens has been "The Pharmacy America Trusts" and has made a reputation on quality products, customer service and convenience. Now, millions of people are putting their trust in Walgreen Brand products with our 100% satisfaction guarantee. We hope you continue to purchase Walgreens Brand products that are backed up by our quality guarantee. Again, thank you for writing. I hope you will continue to purchase our products, and if I may be of any further help to you, please feel free to contact me.

Sincerely, Lynn D.
Consumer Relations Representative Product Quality Concerns

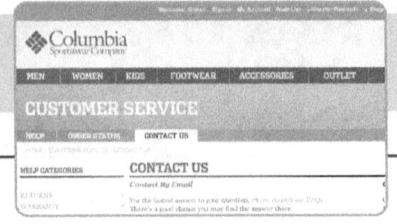

Columbia,

I wanted to write to you to tell you that Columbia clothing saved my life!

Last Christmas while taking a rather speedy hayride, a large bump in the road dislodged me from the back and sent me careening down an icy hillside slope and into the dark abyss of the lonely and unforgiving wilderness.

The temperatures dropped rapidly! I feared for my life out there in the snowy unknown. The wind picked up and the wildlife began calling as if they knew a fallen victim was in their vicinity, waiting to become their dinner.

I walked in the deep snow what seemed like for days, drinking my own urine and eating pinecones for sustenance. Luckily I had on a Columbia jacket or I don't think I'd have made it through the night.

When the morning came, I used the sun to guide me back to the lodge where I proceeded to consume eggnog and bacon till the feeling came back into my face.

Thank you all for your great outerwear. I'd be lost without it!

Norman Willy Frillman

Hello Norman,

Thank you for contacting us! That sounds like it was quite the trip! I don't think I will be taking any winter hay rides anytime soon after hearing about this. I am glad to hear that you were impressed with our gear, and I am even more delighted to hear how it helped you survive through the night.

If you think the gear you have now is awesome just wait until you get a chance to try out our new Omni-Heat technology. Designed for the rugged greater outdoors it is full of these cool reflective dots on the inside of that jacket that reflect back the heat your body generates.

I also would like to know if you would be interested in some Columbia stickers. It would be a great way to show your pride of our gear and I would love to mail some to you. Please let me know if you would be interested.

Regards,

Michael
Customer Care
Columbia Sportswear Company

SENT

CONTACT US

QUESTIONS? COMMENTS? SUGGESTIONS?

Feel free to contact us by filing out the form below.

Dear Hawaiian Tropic,

I recently returned from a vacation in Puerto Peludas, Mexico. While I was there I used your Dark Tanning Oil SPF0 sun screen product and ended up getting horribly burned!

My friends and I went on a day long boat trip out on the open water to go scallop hunting and I used your Coppertone Dry Oil sunscreen number 4 the whole time and at the end of the 11 hour day, I was scorched from head to toe!

I thought your sunscreen was supposed to give the best sun protection of any other sunscreen? I ended up having to stay in the shade the rest of my vacation. I was really disappointed because I hadn't been in the sun for about six years and was really looking forward to getting more time in the hot Mexican sun.

What do you recommend I do the next time I go on vacation?

N Willy Frillman

REPLY

Dear Willy,

Thank you for taking the time to e-mail us with your comments and questions about our Hawaiian Tropic Sun Care products.

We appreciate your input, as we are committed to manufacturing the highest quality line of sun care products.

The Skin Cancer Foundation recommends SPF's of at least 15, which block 93% of UVB. While SPF's higher than 30 block 4% more UVB. Most broad-spectrum sunscreens and sunblocks with an SPF of 15 or higher do a good job against UVB and short UVA rays. If you are fair skin or in a very warm area such as Mexico, I would recommend at least a SPF30 or higher. The tanning oil, SPF0 has no sun screen in it and will not protect you from sunburn. Please view our Hawaiian Tropic website or other sun sites for more information regarding Sun Protection.

If you have any additional comments or questions, please feel free to email us at http://hawaiiantropic.com/Contact-Us.aspx or call us at (888) 310-4290 between the hours of 8 a.m. and 7 p.m. Eastern Standard Time.

Sincerely,

Patty
Hawaiian Tropic
Consumer Affairs

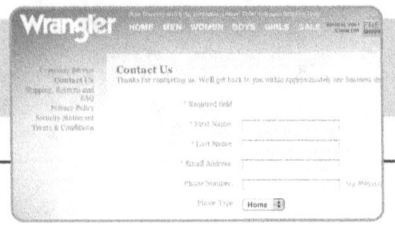

Wrangler

I love the toughness of wrangler jeans. I have to admit that i would not have worn them unless I saw Brett Favre wearing them.

I lived in Africa for a number of years wrangling rhinos and went through jeans like tigers woods went through porn stars, but I've never worn jeans as good as these Wranglers.

I figured once I saw my hero Brett Favre wearing them I'd give them a try. They were a perfect fit! And comfortable! I broke into the Bronx Zoo and tried to wrangle a rhino to give them a proper test, but I was arrested before I even got to the zebras. Even though I didn't wrangle a rhino, the cops chased me around the entire African section. It took six men the get me down, and once they did they beat the hell outta me.

I'd say it was a first class test of the jeans' ruggedness. Nothing compared to what Brett goes through on a Sunday, but still... I tried to call Brett Favre to see if he could bail me out, but he'd already left New York for Minnesota.

Anyway, love the jeans. Classy move on Favre as spokesman. Do you have his phone number or address? I'd love to contact him.

Thanks!

Norman "Willy" Frillman

REPLY

Dear Norman "Willy":

Thank you for your email expressing your feelings about Wrangler products. I'm glad to hear you recovered from your beating.

At Wrangler, we are constantly striving to produce top quality garments at reasonable prices that give our consumers complete satisfaction. Emails such as yours make us feel that our efforts are producing the superior results we are determined to achieve.

If we can ever help you in any way concerning our garments, please let us know. We appreciate you taking the time to write.

Kind Regards,
Eve Birkholz
Wrangler Consumer Relations
1-888-784-8571

Radio Shack,

I love your store and all your fine products, but don't you think the name Radio Shack is a bit dated? I think it's time to upgrade your name. I mean, nobody listens to the radio anymore and shacks are, well, they are the most downtrodden means of living arrangements.

What about Television House? That's pretty good! Or you could go the opposite of Radio Shack and call yourselves Internet Mansion. Internet is the new radio and a Mansion is the opposite of a shack.

What about Hi-Def Castle? Castles trump mansions. They're huge! And everything is Hi-Def. Feel free to use any of these suggestions. Maybe go as big as possible. What's the biggest rage now? 3D? How about calling yourselves 3D Pentagon? The Pentagon is huge! Or maybe 3D Hi-Def Taj Mahal…

Thanks for reading!

Norman Willy Frillman

REPLY

Thank you for taking the time to e-mail us. We appreciate your input and we will forward your suggestions to the appropriate department.

Thank You
Oscar
Customer Escalation Team

Icy Hot,

After I pulled my glutes during the 17th Annual Flogging of the Homeless in Boston this past Christmas, I've been using Icy Hot packs and they're a big help to me. I'm fascinated by the technology. First they're cold and then they get hot. LOVE it!

How does this work exactly? Is it by chemicals? Does the stuff inside actually catch on fire and then turn into ice? What kind of sorcery is this?

Anyway, I have everyone I know using the stuff whether they need it or not. I find that it's good for all kinds of ailments – headaches, hangovers, hunger, depression, boredom, hangnail, sweet tooth, flat feet, tennis elbow, badminton knuckle and could possibly solve world peace... OK, that last part is not true, but if everyone had access to Icy Hot, it may solve a lot of problems.

Thanks for this product. At next year's Flogging I plan to bring a giant suitcase filled with these Icy Hot packets and place them all over my body. That and a few shots of whiskey are just what the doctor ordered...

Thanks a boat load!

Norman frillman

PS: Maybe you could sponsor next year's Flogging event?

Thank you for contacting Chattem, Inc. We are delighted to hear how well the product works for you. If you would like to submit a sponsorship proposal for next year's event, please email the information to me and I will forward it to the Marketing Department for review.

Thank you,

Dawn Simpson
Manager, Consumer Affairs
Chattem, Inc.

Dear Off,

While spelunking in the Adirondack Mountains a few weeks ago, I was viciously attacked by mosquitos the entire time even though I used your OFF Deep Woods insect repellent multiple times during the trip.

What I don't understand is why it didn't work even after I drank more than enough to repel them. I must have sprayed it in my mouth 50 times during the course of one day without any effect whatsoever.

Everyone in my party remained bite free, while I endured unbearable amounts of itchy bites, which I think may have contributed to my dizziness and nauseous feelings. Perhaps I got West Nile Virus, I don't know. But I still feel weird and am thinking of going to the doctor soon.

Please get back to me over this issue and if you know anything about West Nile Virus or any other mosquito induced diseases.

Thank you,

Norman Willy Frillman

Dear Norman,

Thank you for contacting our Consumer Relationship Center. We are sorry to hear of your recent experience following your use of Deep Woods OFF!. We take any report of an adverse experience involving any of our products very seriously.

So that we may best assist you and answer any questions you may have, please contact one of our health care professionals by calling 1-866-231-5406 and provide them with your reference number for your inquiry - 726139. We are available to assist you 24 hours a day, 7 days a week.

Thank you again for contacting us.
Greg Y.

Hi Greg,

Thanks for your response.

I'm unable to call as I don't have use of my ears right now. For some reason in the past few days my ears stopped working and I have a terrible ringing in my ears and pain in my head. I'm going to the doctor in a few days to have it checked out, and try to figure out what the cause of it might be.

When I'm able to hear and see better, I will contact the number you provided and get to the bottom of my OFF problem as I'm planning a trip to the Everglades in July and really need to keep the bugs away.

Thanks a bunch!

Norman

REPLY

CORRESPONDENCE ENDS

Cracker Barrel,

I'm a HUGE fan of your famous reataurants! I'm crazy about Cracker Barrel and the store as well! While visiting relatives, I ate just about every meal there! Love the Meat Loaf!!

Since I love to cook, I began to wonder what other delicious items and toppings you could offer your customers. Have you considered Venison? What about baconnaise?

Here's a list of other things you could offer… flax seeds, turnips, wheat grass, peanut burgers, fried lemons, dandelion stems, mint, cayenne pepper, wheat gravy, baby corn, fluffernutter, tomato pancakes… really the list is endless.

What about trying other kinds of meats? Like say, tongue or lamb fries? People really like exotic meats, especially folks from New York. Things like chopped liver and Llama skin. You could also try frog legs, pickled herring, pork cheek, shark fin, turkey lips, fox kebobs and spam chops.

Some of my favorite things to cook are bologna teriyaki, ostrich chow mein, liver pot pie, alligator hash, ram chowder, oysters benedict, sweet n' sour armadillo, octopus loaf, spicy bone marrow dumplings, turtle, dove, partridge and pear salad.

I have more recipes and ideas so feel free to contact me if you're interested.

Thanks,

Norman Willy Frillman

Dear Mr. Frillman,

Thanks for taking time to contact us here at Cracker Barrel Old Country Store. It's always a pleasure to hear from our guests.

We appreciate receiving your recent suggestion. Your comments have been forwarded to the appropriate department for review and consideration.

Again, thanks for the suggestion. We look forward to hearing from you again soon.

Sincerely,

Pam Seay
Guest Relations Representative
Cracker Barrel Old Country Store, Inc.

ESPN,

I'm a huge fan of your channel and magazine and all the content!

I'm new to the internet (just got it a few weeks ago with my computer and rooter) and I'm loving ESPN.com! It's awesome! Up to date news and great funny stuff!

I love page two and all those guys!

I really love Jimmy Traina and the Hot Clicks section. Love all the stuff he posts (videos, websites, articles etc.) and think you got yourselves a good man there! Extra Mustard is REALLY funny! Plus he posts pictures of pretty ladies - and that ain't so bad!! "_=

I'm glad to hear Jimmy has gotten over his Hoof and Mouth Disease and the swelling is now gone.

Thanks and I'll keep on clickin'!!!

Norman Frillman

PS: When is the Swimsuit Issue coming out?

Dear Norman,

Thank you for contacting us.

We value feedback from our fans and thank you for your kind words and support. We will be sure to share your positive feedback with the appropriate department.

For live assistance with this or any other issue, please call Customer Care at 1-888-549-3776 (ESPN) between 8:00 a.m. and 1:00 a.m. EST.

Regards,

Sean
ESPN.com Customer Care

Hi Sean,

Thanks for the response! I was wondering if you'd sent my email to the appropriate department and what they thought of it. I'm new to the internet world and get very excited to know people are reading my emails. Especially Jimmy Traina. He's very handsome.

Where are you guys located? In New York City?

If so, do you have a tour? Any jobs?

Thanks!

Norman Frillman

Dear Norman,

Thank you for your reply.

All the feedback we receive is documented and passed to the necessary departments. The link below is to the FAQ page. This page will assist you in answering your remaining questions. If you need any further assistance please contact us again.

http://sports.espn.go.com/espn/news/story?page=help/espn-faq-postsubmit

For live assistance with any other issue, please call Customer Care at 1-888-549-3776 (ESPN) between 8:00 a.m. and 1:00 a.m. EST.

Regards,
Katy

CORRESPONDENCE CONTINUES

Hi Katy,

Thanks so much for the response. I'd really like to get in touch with Jimmy Traina if that is all possible. I believe he was going to offer me a job on Hot Clicks and I've been getting the runaround a little and I don't feel it is very nice or professional.

If you could perhaps get me his contact information, I'd really appreciate it.

We met a few weeks ago at a Spanish karaoke bar called El Capitan & Tennillo and he gave me his card. I contacted him, we discussed a job, then nothing. I'm a little confused by all this.

Sincerely,

Norman Frillman

REPLY

Dear Norman,

Thanks for writing.

You can write ESPN talent at the address below:
    ESPN
    Attn:
    ESPN Plaza
    Bristol, CT 06010

They do not have public e-mail addresses.

Sincerely,

Chris
ESPN Viewer Response

CORRESPONDENCE CONTINUES

Hi Chris,

Let me get straight to the point. Jimmy Traina owes me money. After an all night bender at the pirate bar 'Anchor and the Fang' he awoke the next day and put on my pants and has since been using my credit cards and charging outrageous items like foot massages and fig sponge baths catered by young men and it's SICK!

If i don't have recourse soon I'll be forced to obtain a lawyer!

Norman Frillman

REPLY

Dear Norman,

Thank you for your reply.

I apologize for any frustration. Unfortunately, we have provided you with the only contact information available for our personalities. You would need to contact him using those means.

If you have any further questions, please feel free to contact us via telephone or email. We are happy to assist you.

For live assistance with this or any other issue, please call Customer Care at 1-888-549-3776 (ESPN) between 8:00 am and 1:00 am EST.

Regards,

Nic Samuelson
ESPN.com

Nic,

Thank you for your time. I called the number provided and apparently Jimmy Traina has left the state with a man named Ricardo W. Tweed and is passing bad checks all over the place. He's basically leaving a trail of heartache and suffering as the police uncover more clues.

I'm meeting with detectives now and giving them detailed information about his identity and possible aliases, many of which belong to your respectable and highly honored colleagues. I pray none of them have been burned as badly as I have.

Hopefully he won't gain employment anywhere else and will be captured soon and given the stiffest of penalties. With all I've been through, I hope it's the death penalty.

All the best,

Norman Frillman

REPLY

Dear Norman,

Thank you for your reply.

I apologize for all the confusion. Jimmy Traina is not employed by ESPN. He is employed with Sports Illustrated as the senior producer for SI.com. Please contact Sports Illustrated for any contact information regarding Jimmy Traina.

Regards,
Sean
ESPN.com Customer Care

CORRESPONDENCE ENDS

Dear Fox Sports,

I wanted to write and say I'm a big fan of your channel and website, but I'm really not too happy with this new writer that you gave his own website to, this Grant Land person.

> Editor's Note:
>
> Grant Land is in reference to Grantland, "The Sports Guy" Bill Simmons' defunct sports and pop culture website produced by ESPN.

I realize that folks enjoy other things besides sports and news, but this Grant Land jerk has all kinds of stuff posted that I don't like. Things like movie reviews, videos of You Tube filth and other raunch.

And not only that, he uses filthy language that I don't care for. He also uses big words that I find difficult and forces me to look in the dictionary to completely understand.

My son reads this Mr. Grant's stuff and I don't like him reading curse words. My son is only 22 and he shouldn't be reading the F-word and other foul language words.

I already read this dummy Jimmy Traina on S.I. and his raunch going on, plus ESPN and their filth, so I don't understand why you gave a whole entire website dedicated to Grant Land's dirty satanic thoughts and his disgusting filthy raunch.

Sincerely,
Norman Frillman

Hello Norman,

You have mistaken us for ESPN. You will need to contact them with your issue.

Thanks again for visiting FOXSports.com.

All the best,
Bret
FOXSports.com Customer Support Team

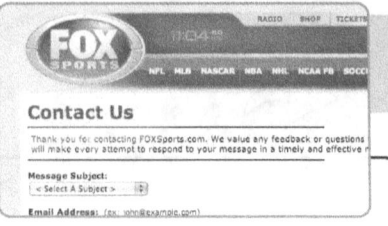

Hello Bret,

Thanks so much for contacting me about this issue. Are you a big fan of Bret Favre like me? (you probably get that a lot!)

I apologize for confusing you guys for ESPN. That was a horrible mistake on my part. The truth of the matter is I don't care for much of anything those ESPN guys do. I think they're all a bunch of jerks, especially that new Grant Land guy they got working over there at the station and on the website. Nothing but a cheap filth monger.

I'm embarrassed I got you guys confused. Sorry! Fox is a great station with fine programming. I love the Joe Buck and Troy Aikman show. Those are real Americans doing fine work!

I was wondering if you could forward my letter to ESPN telling them how much I dislike them and Grant Land and his filth?

I've had problems with them in the past and I may be on the watch list. Do you have their phone number over there? Feel free to call.

Best, Norman

Please let me know if you can write them for me!

REPLY

Norman,

Thank you for your support of FOX Sports and FOXSports.com. We hope you sign up for a FOXSports.com account, and check out our fantasy games, including our new and improved 2011 FOX Fantasy Football game:

http://msn.foxsports.com/fantasy/football/commissioner/

However, we do not have the contact information for ESPN to send your complaint to.

Thanks again for visiting FOXSports.com.

All the best,
Bret
FOXSports.com Customer Support Team

CORRESPONDENCE CONTINUES

Hi Bret,

I appreciate the effort. I will call ESPN myself. Thanks.

Can I have them call you guys? Perhaps you can speak to them, Bret.

Thanks for the Fantasy Information. I will try your improved system. It sounds better than the other one I already use through InStyle magazine. Last year I came in last place in my fantasy team and I lost $5,000 to Kim Kardashian.

Let me know if ESPN can contact you.

Norman

REPLY

Norman,

Unfortunately, we cannot assist any further with this issue.

Thanks again for visiting FOXSports.com.

All the best,
Bret
FOXSports.com Customer Support Team

CORRESPONDENCE CONTINUES

Bret,

I've called ESPN and had a lengthy and heated discussion about their filthy content and overall horrible intentions. I told them how you and I felt about their website, Mr. Grant's terrible language and that idiot Jimmy Traina. Things were said that I regret and lots of filthy things were yelled. Words like filth, dirty, Satanic, French and other terrible things.

As it turns out they may sue us for libel & slander and other things that I can't quite understand.

I've contacted a lawyer. Peter Stallone. He's very available. I've mentioned your name as a witness. We need to meet with them soon and perhaps we can convince them not to sue and maybe change their overall content. Do you live in the greater New York area?

Let me know your availability.

Norman

REPLY

Editor's Note:

Bret did not respond.

CORRESPONDENCE ENDS

Yankee Candle,

I recently received a lovely gift of your scented candles and I simply love them. All kinds of Holiday scents like Christmas tree and Mistletoe and they really enhance the season. I also burned a candle that smelt like Pumpkin Pie and it was so scrumptious that my neighbors thought I was cooking pies! LOL!

I had an idea about other scents you may consider for your candles. Perhaps things like turkey dinner or chicken pot pie would really kick up the appetite! I know you have scents of vanilla and cinnamon, but what about bacon or coffee & toast?

Since we just had relatives over and it was so joyous, I just started jotting down scent ideas on a pad. Things like: scotch & soda, French toast, tipsy uncle, banana daiquiri, bone, fireplace ash, burnt rubber, new car smell, burning house, sexy fireman, Belgian beer, sore muscle cream rub, roast beef au jus, quiche, sorority party, grandmother's chair, honey baked ham, Grateful Dead cousin, rusty metal, clay, pink lipstick, flannel pajamas, flash light, Jaeger shots, tuna fish and cold pizza.

If you are at all interested in these ideas, please feel free to use them. I have plenty more if you'd like me to send them in.

Thank you and have a great day!

Norman Frillman

REPLY

Dear Norman,

Thank you for taking the time to write to us with your comments and suggestions regarding our fragrances. I am happy that you enjoyed them.

If we can be of any further assistance, please do not hesitate to contact us.

Sincerely,

Diane A.
Customer Loyalty Team Yankee Candle Co.
1-877-803-6890 www.yankeecandle.com

Retail Stores Comments & Questions

Share your thoughts.
Please use this form to contact us about Starbucks retail stores. Please read our frequently asked questions.

May we contact you?
Please leave your name, address, phone number and email if you want us to respond to your comments.

Dear STARBUCKS Coffee,

Let me start by stating what a jerk I am! For the longest time I avoided Starbucks coffee thinking that it was an elitist brand without taste or value to the consumer. Well let me tell you have I been mistaken! I went in yesterday and had a cup of your rich, delicious coffee and I was over the moon! WOW! What an error in judgment on my part!!!

I can't believe I waited so long to have your coffee! What an idiot I am! I wasted years drinking inferior coffee while your scrumptious mountain grown coffees lay just feet away from my apartment and my office and my subway station and my bagel place and my gym and my favorite bar. I'm really stupid for this ongoing blunder! I've done some pretty dumb things in my day – eating a whole bucket of mayonnaise, dipping my testicles in a piranha tank – but this oversight takes the cake!

Today I drank 9 cups of Starbucks coffee! I just could not stop drinking it! SOOOO GOOOOOOD! They say that drinking too much coffee is not good for you, but they say you shouldn't eat raw meat and I do that constantly. Now a survey just came out that says coffee may prevent cancer! Can you believe that? I'm going to drink more now than ever before! My heart palpitates a little after cup number 5, but that's OK. I can handle it. I have a strong heart and I feel great after having eliminated cheese and cigarettes from my diet.

Just want to say that this here jerk (Me) is no longer blind to your fantastic coffee and you have a new loyal customer for life!

Thanks a bunch!

Norman "Willy" Frillman

REPLY

Hello Norman,

Thanks so much for contacting us and taking the time to share your thoughts! I'm glad you enjoyed our cofffee. I hope you continue to enjoy your Starbucks visits.

I sincerely appreciate your comments and hope you will continue to enjoy Starbucks coffee.

Sincerely,

Michael V.
Customer Relations
Starbucks Coffee Company
800 23-LATTE (235-2883)
Monday through Friday, 5AM to 6PM (PST)

 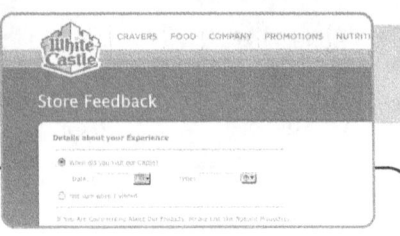

Dear White Castle,

I recently went into one of your establishments and I want to tell you it was TOP NOTCH! The restaurant was clean and the staff was incredibly friendly! I was waited on by a very nice young man. I think his name was Chris Manager. He smiled and made me feel very welcome when I came into the restaurant. I don't see very well, so he was kind enough to help read some of the items on the menu and describe what they were. I had fried fish. It was TOP NOTCH! I couldn't believe that it was what people call "fast food". I felt that the quality of the food was very high. And the flavor! What kind of fish is it that is in those fish sandwiches? Is it tuna or lobster? Whatever it is, it is a little bit of heaven. And it came with some of that tartar sauce on it, which was the icing on the cake! I'd like that tartar sauce recipe.

I also found the fried potatoes to be top notch as well. They had a nice salty coating on them. I'm not supposed to eat too much salt because my doctor said it's bad for my bleeding pancreas, but once in a while a little salt is OK.

I plan on returning to this particular Restaurant and having lunch again. If your staff is half as nice as that guy that helped me, then you have no worries with customer satisfaction I can tell you that right now! I'm from a time when a smile and a firm handshake got you far. You get more bees with honey than with vinegar. That's what I always say.

The bathrooms there were also TOP NOTCH! Very clean and stocked with paper towels and toilet paper and the soap dispenser had plenty of soap. I hate when I use the toilet and there's no soap. It makes me so mad. There's nothing worse than wiping your hands on your pants after you rinse them. I was at one of your 'competitors' once and there was feces on the bathroom floor! That's not the way to run a business!

A NEW loyal customer!

Mr. Norman "Willy" Frillman

SNAIL MAIL REPLY

July 29, 2010

Norman Frillman
402 E. St., Apartment 18
New York, NY 100

Dear Norman Frillman:

Thank you for your recent comments regarding the products and service you have received at our restaurants directed to our corporate office. We always enjoy hearing from customers who enjoy White Castle and its products, especially when they can give us positive feedback. We know your time is limited and your schedule is busy, and so we truly appreciate customers like you, who take the time to let us know when we have done something right. To receive promotional information periodically, please go to our website and sign up for our email list.

Thank you again for your interest in White Castle.

Sincerely,

Elizabeth Ingram

Re: 5855842

CUSTOMER SERVICE CENTER
P.O. Box 725489
ATLANTA, GA 31139-9923

Norman Frillman
402 E. St., Apartment 18
New York, NY 100

Dear Norman Frillman:

CK

My brother Steve has turned me on to your great underwear and since that day, I've had a much better dating life.

I tried other name brand underwear but I didn't think they were comfortable. I won't mention the company's names, but one has a famous basketballer as a spokesman (huge and baggy in the seat) and the other looks like a math problem (their briefs ware like packing sausage in a skin and cut off the circulation to my legs).

I confided in my brother Steve that I was lacking confidence and not fitting into my jeans so well in the front. Steve said that I should "Do Calvin's." It makes "your manhood arrive three minutes before you do"... Well, I've since felt more confident wearing your shorts and not only that but they're comfortable as well.

I love how I feel and look in these and my jeans fill out nicely in the front. All of Steve's friends agree and have all asked me to go out on dates. But I only go one way! Exit only! Haha!

I've had lots of great dates (with women) that Steve has introduced me to and I've even gotten lucky a few times. So next time Sparkle the International Diva or Dougina the Veloci-Rap-Star want to go out again, I'll be confident in saying YES!

Thanks a bunch!

Norman "Willy" Frillman

REPLY

Dear Norman,

Thank you for shopping with cku.com.

We appreciate the time you've taken to share your comments regarding our undergarments. We value any feedback that you can provide, as it helps us to better meet the needs of our customers.

Your comments are definitely welcome and they are taken very seriously. I have taken the liberty of forwarding your feedback to the appropriate department for review. We continue to be committed to providing our customers with the highest standards of service in our industry. You are truly important to us, and deserve the best of what we have to offer.

If there is anything else with which we can assist, please feel free to contact us at any time! We value your business and look forward to meeting your needs again in the future.

Sincerely,
Jeanie Lehman
customerservice@cku.com
1-888-841-4441

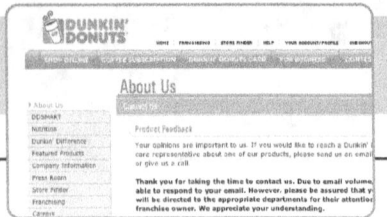

Dunkin Donuts

Dunkin Donuts is pure heaven! I swear on a dozen bibles I love dunkin donuts soo much! I'm ADDICTED to them!

Last week I bought a dozen donuts each morning and ate the whole box myself. Is that wrong? Then on Sunday, my wife went to the movies with a girl friend and I snuck out and got a dozen jellies and scarfed them down before she got home. I think i have a problem! That's 72 donuts in one week! Not to mention the 10 to 15 I snuck in at night! Homer Simpson would be proud! LOL!

She's going out of town for a week on business and I'm afraid what will happen if she's not around! She keeps me in line, but without her, I may go over 100 donuts in one week! Is that a record? Is that healthy? I'm eating a donut as I'm writing this!

Let me know what to do. Do you have any new donut creations coming in the future? I'd like to be a guinea pig...

Did I mention I live around the corner from a DD? When I walk the dog I bop in for 6 or 7 French crullers. One night I actually pretended I had a leg cramp that needed to be walked off so I could hit DD! I put down 8 Boston creams that night. I have problems. Delicious problems. The thing is, I'm not fat, I'm rail thin. My wife hates me! She eats 1 donut and gains 10 pounds I eat non-stop and lose 3. I think it's all going to my heart though. I don't know. I haven't been to the doctor since I was 13. Maybe it's the donuts that keep me healthy...

Ok best to you all.

Norman "Willy" Frillman

REPLY

Dear Norman,

Thank you for taking the time to contact Dunkin' Donuts. It was a pleasure hearing from you today.

We are always happy to hear from customers who love our products and appreciate you letting us know how much you love our donuts.

At Dunkin' Donuts we value our customers and are committed to making your visits to our stores a pleasant experience.

Thank you and have a great day.

Lena
Customer Relations Associate

LOGGED OFF

www.ingramcontent.com/pod-product-compliance
Lightning Source LLC
Chambersburg PA
CBHW072335300426
44109CB00042B/1492